D1005529

with snippets of culinary lore, each essay is an absolute delight to read. As a special trade, she includes recipes for some of the dishes that play starring roles in this book. The perfect choice for readers who enjoy culinary writings by authors such as Laurie Colwin or Elizabeth David. Highly recommended."

—*Library Journal*

"A delightful excursion into the delicious world of contemplating food . . . Lust's mild irreverence, chatty style and sense of history and family make *Pass the Polenta* a book to keep at your fingertips. . . . Like M.F.K. Fisher, the doyenne of contemplative food writing, Lust has enormous respect for her subject, but she has fun with it, giggling now and then."

—*ForeWord* Magazine

PASS THE POLENTA

And Other Writings from the Kitchen

TERESA LUST

BALLANTINE BOOKS • NEW YORK

A Ballantine Book
Published by The Ballantine Publishing Group

Copyright © 1998 by Teresa Lust

www.randomhouse.com/BB/

Library of Congress Catalog Card Number: 99-90619

ISBN: 0-345-43565-6

This edition published by arrangement with Steerforth Press, L.C.

Manufactured in the United States of America

Cover design by Ruth Ross
Cover illustration by Joel Spector

First Ballantine Books Edition: September 1999

10   9   8   7   6   5   4   3   2   1

For Bert

Table of Contents

Introduction

YOU NEED EAT ONLY AN occasional good meal, or spend a very long stint eating nothing but bad meals, to develop an appreciation for food. Appreciate enough food, and sooner or later you will find yourself up to your elbows in its preparation. From there it is just a short step to realizing food is not merely about calories and minimum daily requirements and metabolic pathways. At its very heart, food is about people. It is an integral part of our social history that has affected our lives since long before Esau traded his birthright for a bowl of lentils.

To say the history of society is the history of hunger is hardly a stretch. We made arrowheads for the hunt, earthenware pots for the gruel. Once we developed wheat and maize, we could settle into communities, and once we created the Spice Road we could roam distant lands to bring delicacies back home. Instead of a shorter route to cinnamon, Columbus found the New World, and now we find ourselves in a country shaped by the likes of Boston tea and Irish potatoes.

All the while there has been someone in the kitchen getting supper ready. Someone chopping parsley, drizzling olive oil over salad greens, rolling out a crust for pie. To repeat these actions today, then, is to establish a bond with a line of cooks that is centuries long and continents wide. And to discover in an ingredient, a culinary technique, or a recipe some new link to the past has deepened immeasurably my appreciation for the art of cooking.

This passion of mine was born at the dinner table in the two-story Cape where my parents still live in Washington State. I soon gravitated to the kitchen counter by my mother's side, where along with my three sisters I learned to make raspberry jam, to roll out sugar cookies, to use the tines of a fork to seal the edges of ravioli.

After I decided the biology degree I received in college had no practical applications whatsoever, I took up cooking as a profession. And after several years now in the restaurant trade, from my home state of Washington to California to New England, I have mixed martinis, bussed tables, drawn espressos, mopped floors, sharpened knives, cleaned calamari, glazed tortes, grilled rib eyes, and plated countless meals. I have had the good fortune to work with a number of devoted, skilled teachers in the professional kitchens where I have worked. What's ironic is that these chefs have helped reveal to me just how much I appreciate the cooking of the home. For dining at the home table creates an intimacy and a communion that no restaurant can ever capture. And cooking in the home kitchen for family and friends brings me a sense of immediacy and reward that I do not quite find in the workplace.

Some time ago, my husband Bert bought a little black book. He decided not to use it for recording names and addresses and the other pertinent facts you find in your average little black book. Instead, he started writing down the dinner meals we cooked together and shared. At first, I found this rather silly, embarrassing even, especially when we entertained, for like a proud papa showing off his baby pictures he would drag out the book and prattle off lists of menus past: sautéed salmon with lemon and chives on a bed of wild leeks; fettuccine with chanterelles, thyme and cream; braised lamb shanks with marsala, whole cloves of garlic and sage.

But now that I've convinced him not to launch into recitations for the guests, I've begun to take as much pleasure in the journal as he does. We read through it, and each entry brings back the day. He says, Remember that asparagus and morel risotto you made? and I recall that twilight fell as we ate, and we watched a lovesick woodcock perform his spring mating dance in the pasture below the house. Another entry calls up my parents' visit one Labor Day. My mother and I picked blackberries, and I made a custard sauce to pour over them. Now I can just hear her saying, "Teresa, why didn't you save your egg whites? That's a shame, you know, throwing egg whites out like that, they'll keep in the fridge for a week." Today I realize I wouldn't have needed a reminder if I, too, had lived through a war on ration cards and gas coupons.

In order to share my enthusiasm for cooking with others, I long contemplated writing a regular cookbook. But to speak only in terms of a cup each of carrots, celery, and onions, diced and browned in butter, seemed dreadfully inadequate. Each recipe evoked a remembrance, each ingredient had a tale to tell. So I took a different tack. It appeals to the cook in me to describe the result as two parts memoir, one part recipe collection, one part natural history, and a pinch each of culinary trivia and personal meditation.

At a glance, the topics I've chosen for my essays might seem an odd mix, but they do have common threads. From a pot of polenta, to a crock of sauerkraut, to a dish of strawberry shortcake, they are products of my heritage. They reflect my mother's Italian lineage, my father's German one, and my own

American upbringing, and I have been unabashedly opinionated in their treatment. From the chanterelles on the banks of Mascoma Lake to the apple orchards in the Yakima Valley, my subject matter connects me to locations I hold dear — places I often took for granted until I packed my bags and moved away from them. And from my grandmothers, to my mother, to a persnickety, wizened woman at the grocery store, my essays stand as tributes to people who have shaped my notions about food and the table. You'll find this group includes a preponderance of old ladies, for the cookstoves of my world — and of history, for that matter — have been manned predominantly by women.

So what I conceived at the outset as a collection of recipes turned into a celebration of those who have given meaning and dimension to my cooking. My mentors are ordinary folk, all of them, going about their daily business of baking bread and pouring hearty wine. The ingredients they use are not exotic, their techniques are not complex. Yet as they stand over the stove, they manage to do so very much more than just prepare a meal. They taught me that cooking is an expression of art and of love, of family and self, of the soil and the seasons. I lift my glass to them all.

Pass the Polenta

THE POLENTA STORY is my mother's story, really. "Did I ever tell you about the first time your father had polenta?" she begins, every time she serves it. And I recall her story every time I see polenta on the menu of some trendy, upscale restaurant where I can't afford to dine. Chefs across the country are currently smitten with polenta. They dress it up with all sorts of fancy ingredients — serve it grilled, with sautéed foie gras and Sauternes, for instance, or fried, with seared filet mignon and shaved white truffle, always at a premium price. The most sophisticated diners in the country eat tiny portions of polenta off gold-rimmed Spode china plates, then rinse their palates with Clos-de-Vougeot Burgundy sipped from Waterford crystal goblets.

Yes, when American chefs call it by its Italian name, polenta, it undergoes some sort of transformation. So chic. Exotic. Expensive. This is quite a jump in social status for a dish that in Georgia they call cornmeal mush. Yet back in Italy polenta has always been a staple of the poor. Peasants harvested corn in the fall and air-dried the cobs in their husks over the winter. In the springtime, they milled the ripe kernels into the stone-ground meal that formed the staple of their diet. My Italian grandmother Teresa, who counted me as her namesake, would say an extra rosary if she were still alive to see such pauper fare put on a pedestal. Polenta of all things! What's worse, those pricey restaurants are serving leftovers. Creamy polenta sets up firmly as it cools. Slices of polenta, floured and fried, are what you do with last night's dinner!

Of course it's entirely possible that occasionally some Piedmontese peasant would have unearthed a handful of precious truffles from beneath an oak tree on the way in from the fields. And indeed, his wife might have happily scattered thin slices of these gems over the evening's polenta. But more likely, he ate his dinner with nothing more than a drizzle of melted butter and a few fresh sage leaves.

Polenta is family food. Warm to the mouth, creamy to the tongue, soothing to the throat, and filling to the stomach. Mama feeds it to her baby when his teeth are coming in. Papa feeds it to his mama when her teeth have fallen out. You feed it to the sick because it's bland. You feed it to the poor because it's cheap. When you're lonely, you feed it to yourself because it reminds you of home.

But what you do not do with polenta is serve it to your special guests. That much, Teresa knew on the late autumn evening in 1959 when my mother and father, little more than newlyweds, showed up at her back door in Yakima, Washington. At the time, my parents lived near Seattle, 142 miles away. Just close enough so that after my father's Saturday classes at the university they could decide to load up the car and head east through Douglas fir forests over Snoqualmie Pass. They sped down the sagebrush studded eastern slopes of the Cascades, into the Yakima Valley and up the hill on 23rd Avenue, arriving at the Picatti family kitchen table at seven-thirty, precisely as my grandparents unfolded their napkins across their laps for dinner.

Now, Teresa was not one bit unaccustomed to this. Quite the contrary. Her five children might have all moved out of that redbrick house, but not one of them ever left home. One, or another, or all of them showed back up like boomerangs, usually around mealtime. Consequently, Teresa never unlearned the habit of cooking for a crowd. Why cook one little chicken breast when the pot is big enough for two whole chickens? Not hungry? You must be sick. Eat this, you'll feel better. No one entered Teresa Picatti's kitchen without getting fed.

And yet, when my parents walked through the back door into the kitchen that evening, Teresa was not only surprised, she was mortified. No, she hadn't overcooked the meal, and her larder was far from empty. Why, she'd sliced, minced, and braised in quantities sufficient to feed even four more Picattis should they come to call. But my father was a relative newcomer to the family. A guest for whom Teresa would have arranged a proper feast, even if he was a Protestant. And she knew his tastes were rare indeed, since he had made a bride out of her young daughter. Tonight, what misfortune, all she had for dinner was stew and polenta.

Teresa put her napkin down and stood up from the table. "So good to see you. Come in, come in. Sit down. Oh, but I'm so sorry. If I'd only known you were coming. I've nothing but this old stew on the stove." She clasped her hands together and wrinkled her aquiline nose in a frown. "Well, we can't 'ave this. It justa won't do. Let me fix you a steak, Jim." She turned to my grandfather. "Joe, grab your 'at. Run and pick up a steak for Jim at the market." No matter that the neighborhood grocer had locked his door hours earlier.

Both my grandfather and my mother knew that Teresa was coming undone. She didn't misplace her *h*'s and *a*'s unless she became terribly excited. Teresa had packed her bags and taken ship for America to become a governess when she was just fifteen. After forty-five years in a western agricultural town she'd lost most of her Italian accent.

"Oh, Mom," said my mom. My grandparents had raised her to be an American. The only obvious traces of her heritage were her long, Mediterranean nose, and the same dark hair and olive complexion as her mother. "Don't be ridiculous. We're fine. He'll like polenta." She brought two more place settings to the table. "Besides, we're starving."

"It's a good dinner you've made," said my grandfather Joe. "We should sit and eat."

Teresa relented. "Well, I suppose you're right. I guess it would be a shame to let it go to waste."

The rustic nature of the meal owed as much to its peasant origins as it did to the family-style manner in which it was served. Dinner waited at the table in three dishes: a pot of stew, a bowl of polenta, and a plate of cheeses. Diners assembled their own plates unless they were uninitiated, a guest, or, in my father's case, both. Teresa took his plate and began to dish up. She heaped a mound of polenta onto the middle of his plate. It had taken her about thirty minutes of semi-attentive stirring to make such creamy, smooth polenta. Many cookbooks say the only way to avoid lumps is to drizzle the corn-meal into boiling liquid so slowly you can see individual grains falling from your fingers. But there is an easier way. My grandmother started with four parts *cold* liquid in a heavy saucepan. Perhaps she had a little chicken stock and some milk that day, but she would have used plain water in a pinch. She added one part uncooked coarse-ground cornmeal, a generous spoonful of salt, and some cracked black pepper. She whisked this around until it was nice and smooth, then set the pot over a low flame to stir, stir, stir with a wooden spoon. When the spoon stood up by itself in the sauce pot she knew it was done.

At this point, she threw in a few handfuls of freshly grated cheese. She just happened to have a sliver of Parmigiano-Reggiano left from her last visit to Pete DeLaurenti's store in Pike Place Market. This cheese is the queen of Parmesans. Through serendipity or design, the fortunate cows that graze on the clover in the fertile Enza Valley of Reggio produce some of the richest cream in Italy. Flax-colored, nutty-tasting Reggiano cheese ages eighteen months to become the pride of the region. Teresa tried to keep a piece on hand at all times. Any aged, hard cheese would have sufficed — Parmesan or Romano, domestic or imported. As long as it was grated by hand, that is. I'm sure my grandmother would frown on the stale, pregrated variety you find at the supermarket today.

Teresa next reached for the cheese plate. The nice man at the deli always picked her out a good bulbous round of provolone when she stopped there. She draped a thin slice of the young, soft, buttery cheese over the polenta. Next, she picked up a strip of mozzarella. The gift of mozzarella is not so much in its flavor, but the manner in which it oozes into a dish and picks up flavors from the other ingredients. She wished, I imagine, just this once to be back in Italy, so she could at least garnish this modest meal with fresh Italian mozzarella. True mozzarella comes from the milk of water buffaloes. Italians also make a less expensive, but less flavorful version from cows' milk. Both are extremely perishable, and I doubt my grandmother could find them after she left Turin. She would be pleased to know that fresh mozzarella, both domestic and imported, is now readily available in this country. In keeping with the spirit of polenta's humble roots, she probably used some old, commercial product manufactured out in New Jersey. But even rubbery New Jersey mozzarella melted to velvet on her polenta.

She tore a slice of Gorgonzola into pieces and scattered it onto the steaming polenta, flicking her fingers to keep it from sticking to her hands. You often hear that Gorgonzola is the Italian answer to the blue-veined Roquefort cheese of France. While the two are similar in appearance, Roquefort is made from the milk of the ewe, and Gorgonzola is a product of the cow. For centuries, the town of Gorgonzola near Milan was a stopover for herdsmen and their cattle, who migrated down from the Alps to overwinter on the Po River plain. Because these cows were tired from the arduous descent, the cheese the villagers made from their milk came to be called *stracchino di Gorgonzola; stracco* being the word for "tired" in the local dialect. Somewhere in time the adjective was lopped off, but the town of Gorgonzola remains famous for the creamy, blue-mottled cheese. Some people claim its heady flavor, which is not unlike a combination of toasted almonds and urea, is an acquired taste. Others think it stinks. Of course they are absolutely right. It does stink. It stinks in the same manner as some folks claim oysters stink. Yet both bivalve and blue mold boast advocates who extol their praises and consume them with a passion.

I've no idea what my grandmother thought of oysters, but she added a second slice of Gorgonzola, then reached for the ladle in her stewpot. She'd set to work cooking that stew in the early afternoon, though she often made it a day in advance and heated it up just before dinner. The longer sits the pot, the better tastes the stew, she'd say. She started with a couple of pounds of stewing meat, chuck roast, most likely, trimmed off the gristle, cut it into chunks and dredged the pieces in flour. She put a little lump of the fat into her cast-iron pot, rendered it over low heat and added the meat. When the pieces were nice and browned she threw in a cut-up onion, four or five fat cloves of slivered garlic, a bay leaf, some oregano, thyme, and rosemary. After the onion grew limp and translucent, Teresa poured in a few glugs of red wine, saving the last inch in the bottle for my grandfather's glass at dinner.

Into the pot went a jar of the tomatoes she'd put up last August. She covered the stew with a lid and let it cook away softly on the back burner for a couple of hours. She checked the pot occasionally by sticking a finger into the simmering broth for a taste, giving it a stir, and adding water if too much liquid had evaporated. Near the end, she threw in some sliced celery, a couple of carrots, some mushrooms if she had them, maybe a turnip or two. She let the pot bubble gently until the vegetables were tender and the meat had plumb given up, then seasoned the stew with salt and pepper.

The results were the rich, meaty spoonfuls she ladled over the polenta and cheese. Steaming, thick juices blanketed a bed of polenta. Tender meat, caramelized onions, smoky garlic, aromatic herbs, pungent warm cheese. The whole thing was one melting mound of flavors. Teresa finished the plate with a generous sprinkling of Parmigiano-Reggiano and set it before my father.

After my mother and grandparents had fixed their own plates in turn, my father picked up his fork and started to eat. Teresa kept watch out of the corner of her eye. When my father really enjoys a meal, he polishes it off without saying a word. He doesn't bother with conversation until later, it just slows him down. He bent his head with intention over the plate, revealing thin hair where a bald spot would eventually appear. Rising steam from the stew fogged up his thick horn-rimmed glasses. He quickly finished and politely asked for a second helping.

Teresa looked across the table at my grandfather, who gave her a faint, but encouraging nod, then she served my father up another plateful. But she knew she was not out of hot water just yet. She speared a tight button mushroom that had tumbled from her own mound of stew and tried to busy herself, too nervous to eat much. With the mushroom as a mop she swabbed up rivulets of the rich broth. She prodded bits of tomato, pushed aside the overlooked bay leaf, all the while looking discreetly through the bottom of her bifocals at my father. In her experience, if a guest ate only seconds, he had done so merely to be polite. The meal was not so bad that he would refuse a second taste, but perhaps not so well prepared that he would lose sight of his manners. A genuine culinary triumph came when a guest succumbed to the flavorful temptations on the table before him and dove in with abandon for a third helping.

My father couldn't get enough. With an ever so slightly embarrassed grin on his face, he asked for thirds. This time he prepared his own plate. He scooped up the polenta, laid down the cheese, and slathered on the stew. He hesitated a moment, then added an extra slice of Gorgonzola. Teresa raised her eyes and gave a faint twitch of a smile. "Not bad on a cold night, this polenta, eh?"

Indeed, stew with polenta may not be a tuxedo-clad company dish; perhaps it's just dinner. If anything, it serves as a barometer of the economic times. My mother's oldest brother says during the Depression he would stop by my grandfather's shop on the way home from school. If a customer had come in to settle his bills that day, my uncle knew there would be meat on the table with the polenta. During the fifties, when America prospered, one of my aunts remembers my grandmother stirring the polenta and muttering, "Thirteen kinds of cheese you've got in the Fridgedaire, Joe Picatti. You bring home one more and I'm not speakin' to you for a week."

Is it really such a great surprise to see a bowl of porridge take our country by storm? After all, it was with a barley gruel they called polenta in their stomachs that the Roman legions brought the world to its knees. And with polenta in her sauce pot, Teresa brought my father into the family. All we've done, perhaps, is come full circle.

Easy as Pie

YOU WILL NOT LEARN to make a good pie from a French pastry chef. Classically trained chefs can show you how to make napoleons out of buttery, multilayered *pâte feuilletée*. Or they can teach you to beat extra eggs into your *pâte à choux* for ethereal, high-rising *éclairs au chocolat*. And they do have a pastry they fill with sweetened fruit in their repertoire. They call it *pâte brisée*. The name means "broken pastry," which describes the way chefs originally mixed the dough by breaking off bits of it and smearing them across the counter with the heel of the hand. But what French pastry chefs can't teach you is how to make a tender pie dough.

Pies are an American trademark, although not an American invention. The English were making top-crust-only pies of sweet fruits and savory meats and four-and-twenty blackbirds as long ago as the Middle Ages. But American settlers reinterpreted the pie and made it their own. Chefs don't make pies over in France because they don't have pie pans. They have tart pans, so what they make are tarts, and tarts are made with *pâte brisée*. French-trained chefs will scarcely condescend to utter the words "pie dough." They think their cuisine is inherently superior to traditional American cooking. And their prejudices are not unfounded. *Tournedos à la périgourdine* far surpasses our well-done steak with A.1. Sauce. *Salade niçoise* outshines the scoop of tuna salad you'll find nested in an iceberg lettuce leaf at your nearest cafeteria. And dare I even juxtapose a rich steaming cup of French roast with the insipid brew we pour here in America?

But with *pâte brisée* and pie dough, I'm afraid they are mistaken. The ingredients in the two are essentially the same: flour, water, salt, and some type of fat — usually butter or lard, perhaps shortening — yet something gets lost in the translation when the dough is shaped in the hands of a classically trained chef. Yes, pie dough is better off made with old-fashioned American ingenuity.

The difference, I think, is a product of evolution. French chefs have a habit of complicating the simplest task in order to elevate the banal to the extraordinary. The tenets of French *haute cuisine* emerged back when professional kitchens teemed with little apprentices. The wealthier the château, the more servants who had nothing better to do than stand around all day and seed grapes or beat egg whites. Chefs in large kitchens developed a penchant for complex, labor-intensive cooking techniques to keep their charges from standing idle. They bolstered their egos by creating a cuisine so intricate the plebeians could never duplicate it.

Country farmers' wives perfected the American art of pie baking. Not only did these ladies have pies on their morning agendas, they looked after seven kids, put up a dozen pints of strawberry jam, and finished the laundry before the menfolk returned from the fields for supper. If pies weren't quick and easy to make, they simply wouldn't get made. Pies don't indicate social status, they just taste good.

I did not learn all this until after I accepted a job cooking at a French restaurant. The owner of the place had graduated from Ecole de Cuisine La Varenne in Paris. Her chef graduated from Le Cordon Bleu in London. She taught me, with my meager bachelor's degree in biology, to make heavenly *génoise*. He showed me how to sauté *filet mignon*. A former chef there, a graduate of the New England Culinary Institute in Montpelier, Vermont, helped me perfect my delectable *pommes de terre dauphinoise*.

But I became suspicious when I discovered, despite their diplomas and the miles they had collectively traveled to learn to cook, that they all made pretty lousy pies. La Varenne made a pumpkin pie for the staff one Thanksgiving. Impossibly tough crust. Montpelier once brought an apple pie to the Christmas party. Completely soggy. Le Cordon Bleu, while he made a mean hollandaise, did not do pies. He had, however, once made a pear tart. Burnt. Come to think of it, the chef at a previous job, who was a graduate of the California Culinary Academy, made rather sorry pies himself.

I waited tables at that last restaurant. I once overheard a customer, a genuine pie connoisseur, expound on the virtues of the perfect pie. A limp, half-eaten piece of *tarte aux pommes* — that's apple tart — on the plate in front of him apparently prompted his discussion with a female companion.

The two elements of a pie, he said, are obviously the filling and the crust. The filling must be juicy, but not so runny as to soak the crust. Its flavor tart, but not sour. Sweet, but not cloying. The real cornerstone of a good pie is a tender, flaky crust. A bad crust differs from a great crust in the same manner as a chemist would distinguish a compound from a mixture.

I've given it some thought, and I think I understand what he meant. In a compound, any number of elements are atomically bonded to produce a unique substance from the original components. Salt is an example of a compound: one sodium ion bonds to one chlorine ion to form sodium chloride. In a mixture, various elements combine, coexist harmoniously, yet remain individually distinct. A bowl of salt and pepper is an example of a mixture. Stir it up all you want, you'll still be able to tell one from the other.

Now take pie crusts. Flour, butter, and water are the elements. Processing these ingredients to the point where they form a smooth, homogeneous dough results in what could be thought of as a new compound. The temptation to proceed to this point is strong, since the more you handle the dough, the easier it is to work with. When the flour comes in contact with water, a protein called gluten develops. The more you work the dough, the stretchier the gluten becomes. Development of gluten in a pie crust signals the beginning of the end. To slow this process, some pie bakers add a hint of vinegar or lemon juice to their dough, especially in warm weather when the butter wants to melt into the flour instead of to retain its own identity. The acid in the vinegar helps inhibit the formation of gluten.

The method for making pie dough is diametrically opposed to that of bread baking. A successful yeast bread depends upon vigorous kneading so the dough can expand and trap the gases given off by the yeast. The result is the chewy, heavenly texture of fresh baked bread. Pie dough, lacking the yeast, turns into a pliable piece of cardboard.

What you strive for in pie dough is a sort of gestalt-mixture. Indeed, the whole is greater than the sum of its parts, yet the crux lies in each part retaining a bit of its own identity. The finished product should possess elements of lumpiness and untidiness — chunks of butter, a dusting of unincorporated flour. When you roll the pastry into two dimensions, the butter blobs should appear as distinguishable streaks throughout the dough. During baking the butter melts back into the dough, but the nooks and crannies the chunks occupied are puffed with steam from the evaporating water. *Et voilà!* A flaky crust.

Achieving this end is no small feat. While the customer in the restaurant sounded good in theory, I bet he never tried making a pie crust. Certainly, he would have been more forgiving had his fork ever known the disappointment of facing off with a doughy, sodden crust of his own making. A connoisseur of pies, yes, but a baker of none, I'm sure.

Until recently, I counted myself among those pie bakers who had tried and failed. I knew that baking a good pie was no piece of cake. But still, I harbored hopes that someday I might create a paragon of pie crusts with my own two hands. All of this, perhaps, because some idealist intimated that such a thing could possibly be.

After I started baking for La Varenne I set out on a quest for the perfect pie crust. In my naïveté, the mystical complexities of French baking enthralled me. I pored through La Varenne's library of pastry books. I spent hours jotting down recipes and key instructions: always use lard. Lard is too greasy, use only butter. Use a little cake flour to lighten the dough. Use only pastry flour. Don't touch the dough with your hands, use a food processor. Work the dough with your fingers. Chill the dough twenty-four hours before rolling out. Ready to roll out immediately after mixing.

The more I read, the more overwhelmed I became. So I sought the advice of one of the best pie bakers I knew. I telephoned Nana, my paternal grandmother, on her 350-acre farm in Yakima, Washington. Yakima proudly calls itself the Fruit Bowl of the Nation, and Nana has been wrapping up its bounty in pie crusts for the better part of her eighty years. Rhubarb, strawberry, raspberry, cherry, plum, apricot, peach, blackberry, pear, apple, pumpkin, mincemeat. She's made pie out of all of them.

"Why, honey," Nana said when she heard my voice on the other end of the telephone line. "You do make my day when you call me out of the blue like this."

"Nana," I said, "I'm making a pie and I need some help. I've been reading my cookbooks for instructions, and all it's got me is terribly confused. I think I've written down all the important steps to remember, but I want to see how your recipe compares to all these others."

"I doubt I could know any better than all your cookbook authors, but go ahead," she said.

"They say you should invest in a marble pastry board and rolling pin for the best results in rolling out the dough. Otherwise, you should ice down your countertop to help keep the work surface cool. Do you do that?"

"No, but I make my pies in the morning before the heat sets in."

"Do you use lard? And do you freeze it for forty-five minutes before using?"

"Well, no, just butter and sometimes some shortening. That freezing business might be a good idea, but I'm sure I'd never remember to do it on time."

"What about your flour? Do you use pastry flour, or do you mix one part cake flour with three parts all-purpose?"

"I've never even heard of pastry flour, dear. I just use whatever I've got on the shelf. All-purpose flour, most likely."

"Do you give the dough two turns before you form the pie shell?" I asked.

"What's that?"

"You know, do you roll out the dough, spread it with thin slices of butter, fold it in thirds like a business letter, chill it for half an hour and then repeat the process?"

"Good heavens, child, sounds like you'd be hard at it all day. I suspect all that rolling'd just make it tough."

And so the conversation went. Do you beat the butter with a rolling pin to make it malleable, yet still cool? No. Do you use a food processor to mix the dough? No. Do you roll the dough out between two sheets of waxed paper? Do you chill the dough two hours or overnight before using it? Do you use milk instead of water for a tender crust? No. No. No. So much for the holy writ.

"Well," I asked. "What *do* you do?"

"I don't think there's any need to go to all that fuss," Nana said. "Let me tell you my recipe."

I rummaged through the clutter on my desk for a pen. "Okay, I'm ready."

"Now, you take two and a half cups of flour and put it in a big bowl with a pinch of salt and a bigger pinch of sugar. Stir it around a bit to mix it up. Cut a stick and a half of cold butter into small chunks. Add it to the flour along with a quarter cup of shortening. You can use just butter, that'd be two sticks altogether. The shortening gives a flakier crust, but the butter makes it a bit tastier. It's up to you," Nana instructed. "Do you have a pastry cutter? It's a gem for working the butter into the flour. But if you don't, two forks'll work almost as well. Don't use your hands if the weather's hot. They'll be too warm and you'll melt the butter. What you want to do is cut away at the butter until it's just a bunch of little pieces no bigger than the tiger eye marbles you kids used to play with. Stop mixing before you think it's done. That's the key, really."

I scrawled away as she talked, trying to remember just where I'd ever put those tiger eyes. How nonchalant she was with her pinches of this and that. And here I thought pie making was serious, rigid business.

"You're better off with too many big lumps than too many little ones. Next, take a half cup of ice water. That's one thing I do in advance. I fill a small bowl with cold water and drop a few ice cubes into it. And if it's really hot, I add a teaspoon of vinegar. I don't know why, other than it's what my mama did. Drizzle that ice water over your flour. Save a tad-bit out because you might not need all of it. Stir it in with a fork until it just starts to come together — it should feel like a handful of good, rich soil. Dump the whole works out onto the counter and shape it into two disks with your hands. Here's where you can add some more ice water if it doesn't hold up. Don't worry if it won't all stick. Put the dough into the refrigerator while you make your filling. What kind of pie are you going to make, honey?"

"I picked some blackberries yesterday from the woods behind the house," I said.

"Oh, that sounds real nice. Take your berries, don't wash 'em, it rinses away all their juice. Just pick 'em over a bit. A few leaves and stems are good for the digestion, you know. You'll need about two pints of berries when you're through. Put your berries in a bowl with about three-fourths a cup sugar. A little more if the berries are tart, a little less if they're good and sweet. Add a quarter cup of flour, some cinnamon, and maybe a sprinkle of nut-meg. Squeeze the juice of a lemon over the berries. I sometimes grate the rind first and add it to the berries. Makes it nice and lemony. Stir it together a bit with your hands, then let it set for a while. What you're doing here is giving the juices and the flour time to make a rich, thick syrup."

"How long should I wait?"

"Oh, long enough to wash up the dirty dishes. Then you're ready to make a pie. Here's where I turn the oven on to 350 degrees. Spread some flour on the countertop and roll out your first round of dough."

Hearing Nana's slow, dear voice, I envisioned her in the kitchen, an apron tied around her waist, working away at the counter, a scene I had witnessed many times. Brown-splotched farmer's-wife hands deftly grasp the rolling pin with three fingers apiece. That arthritis has plagued her for years. A brush of flour on her cheek blends into her silver hair.

The disk of dough begins to flatten and spread after a few smooth strokes under the pressure of her rolling pin. Nana slides a spatula under the dough to loosen it from the countertop. She wipes more flour over her work surface, flips the dough over and gives it a 45-degree rotation. This continues until the pastry is a perfect round, twelve inches across and an eighth-inch thick. She folds the dough in quarters, lifts it, and unfolds it into her pie plate.

Nana transforms the second round of dough in like manner. She pours the filling into the pan and dots it with thin flakes of butter. Over the berries she drapes the top crust, folding it in around the bottom layer like she would tuck the edges of a winter quilt around a mattress. She makes a tidy border by pinching the dough between her thumb and the side of her index finger all the way around the rim. Dough clings to the sides of her wedding band. She makes a snowflake pattern of slits in the top crust with the point of a sharp knife to let the steam escape.

"If you like a shiny crust you can brush the top with some lightly beaten egg or milk," she continued. "Put it in the oven for a good hour. I usually put a cookie sheet under my pies. If there's one thing for certain, it's a pie likes to bubble over. All that burned sugar's the dickens to clean off the floor of an oven. When it's golden brown, pull it out of the oven and leave it on the counter to cool. There you have it."

I got started as soon as I hung up the phone. I set a bowl of ice water on the counter and followed her directions precisely. That is to say, I didn't measure much, mix much, or worry much. When I pulled the pie from the oven the mingled aroma of warm berries, browned butter, and Nana's kitchen wafted through the air. The crust had a golden sheen. Its edges revealed distinct, flaky layers where the dough had puffed and expanded. Thick, translucent, purple filling bubbled through the steam vents. It was beautiful.

I was so proud of that pie I took it in to share with my coworkers at the restaurant. I knew I was putting my prize before a panel of tough critics when I walked through the door. La Varenne and Le Cordon Bleu puttered about the kitchen. Coincidentally, Montpelier had dropped in from out of town to visit. Still, I was confident.

La Varenne brought out plates and a knife, cut into the pie, and served it forth. Filling glistened and oozed seductively out the sides of each piece. The three of them stood around me as we ate, alternately taking bites of the pie, then lifting their plates up before their eyes to examine it with closer scrutiny. The crust had cooled to room temperature, but the tart, juicy berries still felt warm on the tongue.

"Oh, God, this is good pie," said Montpelier. "Did you use pastry flour, or part cake flour and part all-purpose? Did you use a food processor?"

"This is truly delicious," said Le Cordon Bleu. "The crust is amazing. So light and flaky. How many turns did you give the dough? Did you use frozen lard?"

"Outstanding!" pronounced La Varenne. "I can't remember tasting such fine *pâte brisée*. Did you use a marble pastry board and rolling pin, or did you ice down the counter?"

La Varenne began to look a bit sheepish. It was her stern policy to refuse all customers' requests for recipes. She regarded them as patented possessions whether they were her own creations or not. "Do you think . . . would you mind . . . could you please give me the recipe for your wonderful *pâte brisée*?"

"Well, I guess I'd be happy to," I said. "But it's not *pâte brisée*. If you want to make a good pie crust, you have to start with pie dough."

A Good Roast Chicken

THE DAY MY GRANDFATHER brought home the Rhode Island Reds is the day my mother learned to be a Singer. You might read this and think I mean *singer,* one who belts out show tunes, but I'm talking poultry plucking here, and I do mean one who singes over an open flame. Her job, she said, when I asked her please to tell me again about her day as a poulterer's apprentice, was to singe the pinfeathers off the chickens once they'd been plucked. She'd rather have been a Waxer, which Mrs. Sebastian down the road, who kept White Leghorns, said was better than being a Singer. Mrs. Sebastian said the pinfeathers slipped right out when you painted the naked birds with melted paraffin and then peeled back the hardened wax. But my grandmother Teresa was saving her paraffin for making grape jelly. Besides, she said, putting up chickens made mess enough without a pot of hot wax underfoot.

A generation and a half later, I pulled a roast chicken from the oven and found myself thinking not of my mother singeing off pinfeathers, but of all the ways I could have prepared my chicken that night. Could have made Chicken Kiev or Chicken Cordon Bleu, Chicken Chasseur or Chaud-Froid. I could have ballottined the breasts and fried the thighs and Buffaloed the wings, or served it up coq au vin'ed, or jambalaya'd or vindaloo'd, but nothing would have captured the simple essence of a chicken quite like my roast.

It was going to be a good one, I could tell. Skin crisp and the color of dark toast, drippings sputtering in the bottom of the pan, and the scent of it like my grandmother's house minus the tomato sauce. You could call it a preparation deceptive in its simplicity. I didn't even use a recipe, just rinsed and patted dry a four-pound roasting hen, brushed it with melted butter and sprinkled it inside and out with coarse salt and cracked pepper. Then I set it breast-side up on a bed of rosemary sprigs in a roasting pan and drizzled it with the juice of a lemon. I tucked the spent lemon inside the bird's cavity along with a few fresh sprigs of thyme and some garlic cloves, and set the pan in a 400-degree oven for an hour or so, until the juices ran clear when I poked it in the thigh. A meat thermometer, if I'd remembered to use it, would have read about 170 degrees. Then I let the roast rest for ten minutes and put it on a platter with some parslied new potatoes and buttered carrots. That's it.

But I'd gone to the farmers' market and sprung for a free-range chicken, one who'd had the run of the barn and eaten a few slugs in its day — a chicken with some real meat on its bones and not some junkie chicken shot up with hormones and antibiotics. The garlic and the potatoes and the carrots came straight from my garden that morning, and the herbs grew in pots on my front porch. It occurred to me that a good roast chicken dinner is not got from a recipe, but from a way of life — a life full of vegetable gardens and barnyards and meals rushed from the farm to the table. By extension — and this is when I envisioned my mother holding a freshly plucked chicken over a candle flame — it is a life where there's no denying that what lies succulent and crisp on a bed of rosemary sprigs once scratched in the dirt.

If you had asked my grandfather Joe as he crated up chickens on an August day now fifty years deep in my mother's memory, he might have added that not only can barnyard birds scratch in the dirt, they can peck like the devil. In fact, some of them, the old biddies, are just too ornery and tough for the roasting pan, and they need a good long simmer in a pot to cook the meanness out of them.

Joe was not a chicken farmer by trade, although he raised a few Banty hens for eggs. An Italian immigrant to Washington State, he worked first as a butcher over in Cle Elum, and then as a ferry-crosser down on the mighty Columbia before he ended up a self-taught electrical engineer in the Yakima Valley — which, he liked to say, just goes to show how far you can get on a little spit and elbow grease. He tended irrigation systems for many of the fruit growers in the area, orchardists who harnessed Cascade Mountain snowmelt to overcome the fact that their rain-shadow valley received only eight inches of precipitation a year.

Joe set out for the orchards that morning to have a look at some farmer's pump. After a brief period of inspection and consultation, he agreed to make the necessary repairs for a fee of seventy chickens. Now, in the cash-strapped wake of World War II the barter system was alive and well in the valley. Joe had been known to take occasional payments in apples or firewood or even cherries. As for live chickens, well, these birds were a first. But why not? he thought, in this life you take what you can get.

When it came time later that day to collect his wage, I like to think my grandfather summed up his efforts and decided the pump just wasn't quite a seventy-chicken job. Or else I imagine him sizing up those birds and finding one of them just wasn't quite up to snuff. But most likely, he simply miscounted, because one of my aunts swears he returned to town at the end of the day with only sixty-nine Rhode Island Reds in the back of his '37 Dodge pickup. And by the way those Rhodies squawked and flapped and carried on, you'd have thought they knew they were off to meet their Maker. Which they were.

It was my grandmother who did them in. She took one hard look at my grandfather and that truck and those birds, and muttered, "Joe Picatti, if I 'adda gun that'd shoot around corners you'd-a been dead long ago." But then she reached for an apron to cover her housedress and set to work right there in the driveway. One after another, she held each plump, wriggling body between her knees and grasped with determined fingers the sweet spot partway up its scrawny throat. Then she administered a sharp, clean yank, up and out just so, which broke the bird's neck and killed it instantly. She never winced. Did not even issue a barely audible gasp; neither as each chicken breathed its last, nor afterward, during those long slow seconds when the dead creature convulsed wildly in her clutch before falling limp.

Don't get me wrong, my grandmother Teresa would much rather have spent her time stirring risotto or counting her rosary or growing scarlet runner beans than snuffing out life. Her comment about the corner-shooting pistol notwithstanding, she wasn't a violent sort, wasn't one to commit what some would call cold-blooded murder with her bare hands. She had to wear gardening gloves — though not so much out of squeamishness, or out of a desire to distance herself from such a disagreeable task, but to keep from getting hangnails. And on that sun-baked afternoon with sixty-nine dead Rhode Island Reds growing warm under her aquiline nose, she would have had no time for explaining the difference between murder and putting dinner on the table.

She and Joe strung the chickens by their feet from the clothesline and let the blood drain out onto the grass. Instead of lamenting the moral implications of the food chain, Teresa promised to fix Joe a mess of cockscombs for dinner that night. Too bad she hadn't any artichokes, for cockscombs and kidneys sautéed with artichokes was the favorite royal feast of none other than Catherine dei Medici. But Teresa would dredge the combs in flour, fry them in the olive oil she saved for special occasions, and that would be feast enough.

Dinner would just have to wait, though, for she had a flock of chickens still to be dressed and drawn. It seems to me a curious fact that while poultry dressing is the sage and cornbread stuffing you eat at Thanksgiving, dressing poultry is what you do when you clean a bird of all its feathers; but so it goes. Teresa put a kettle of water on to boil. She soon had the whole kitchen smelling of chicken soup as she plunged each bird headfirst into the bubbling pot of water and swirled it around for a few seconds until the feathers slipped away without tugging. Two of my aunts, who had been enlisted as the Pluckers, took the dripping birds back to the driveway and plucked out wet feathers by the handful. The feathers dried in the August heat and wafted upward, scattering across the lawn. Feathers hung from the zinnias in the flower bed and caught in between the slats in the picket fence. They clung to my aunts' pedal pushers and my grandmother said, careful now, don't be bringing them in the kitchen.

Next, my mother came in as the Singer. She was a twiggy child of eleven, all knees and elbows and wide brown eyes. She still had a dark, thick head of Shirley Temple curls that summer, and not the flat, limp strands that grew in after her bout a year later with typhoid fever — Grandma warned her what happened to naughty children who went off swimming in the irrigation ditch. Joe lit one end of a tightly twisted newspaper like a torch. He held a naked bird upside down, then showed my mother how to sear off the nubbly pinfeathers and the soft down without charring the skin. When the flame burned down close to his fingers, he dropped the newspaper to the cement driveway and finished the job by turning the chicken over the flame like a roast on a rotisserie spit.

All afternoon my mother singed away. And as she singed, her nose wrinkled up and her lips drew tight and my grandfather said, "Come now, honey, they don't smell that bad. Your face is bound to freeze that way, you keep scrunching up your nose like that." She blushed, handed him another bird to be drawn, and tried to concentrate on the sounds he made while he worked — the smooth scrape of metal on metal every time he honed the blade of his boning knife against his carbon butcher's steel, the knuckle-pop-pop as he snapped off the feet at the knee joint, and the soft slap every time he plopped a chicken on his cutting board. Grandma leaned toward my mother and said, just watching him you'd have thought only a day and not twenty years had passed since he worked as a butcher up in that coal town of Cle Elum. Which was the job, and don't you forget it, that kept him out of the mines.

Sixty-nine times he laid a chicken across the table and ran his knife down the length of its neck. He pulled out the windpipe and the gullet and then the crop, which he split open, revealing to my mother the grains of corn that had been the bird's last meal. He made an incision at the chicken's tail end and extracted the entrails, setting aside the giblets — the liver, heart, and gizzard, that is. He'd always been a shoo-in for giblets in tomato sauce. Occasionally he found a string of yolks inside a laying hen. These he placed in a bowl so that Teresa could whisk them with marsala and a touch of sugar into the custard she called *zabaglione*. But the intestines, which he had never learned to like, not even in a fritatta with cheese, so help him, he threw out with the rest of the viscera. Finally, he scooped out and discarded the oil sac at the heart-shaped base of the tail, the part he called the pope's nose, then handed the bird to one of my uncles, who wrapped it in heavy paper and packed it for the meat locker they rented from the butcher.

I like to linger on this image of my grandfather, of him working with nimble fingers, wielding a knife with a competent hand. His hand, my mother recalls, could take a pocketknife and whittle off the entire skin of an apple in one long strip. As children, she and my aunts would lie sprawled on the floor, mouths agape like nestling sparrows, while he dropped the fleshy peel onto their tongues. He had a stroke just about the time I was old enough to shape my own memories, and in those memories his hand rests on the arm of a green La-Z-boy rocker and squeezes an orange ball, never quite recovering its strength.

I regret not having known my grandfather back when he possessed a hand steady enough to draw a chicken. But I am not so sentimental as to pine for a time when women in starched aprons wrung the necks of chickens out of necessity, no matter how farm-fresh the resulting meal. I find my terra-cotta herb pots, my vegetable patch and my farmers' market chicken a healthy compromise. So does my mother, who never pursued her career as a Singer, and now prefers to leave the unpleasantries of dressing and drawing to the abattoir. Yet she doesn't use her back-then-we-really-had-it-rough voice, the one she uses when she mentions gasoline rationing cards and hand-me-down boys' saddle shoes, when she recounts her day as the Singer. Rather, her voice takes on a warm lilt — if not of nostalgia, than at least of bemusement.

My mother's chicken-singeing tale came back to me just the other day while I waited at the meat counter in the grocery store. Actually, I thought of my grandfather, because I stepped in line behind a woman who made me think the art of sizing up a chicken is still alive and well.

She was a wisp of an old woman, clad in a weathered pea coat and galoshes, and wearing a scarf over her head tied tight underneath her chin. All she wanted, I heard her ask, was five pounds of chicken. Drumsticks with the thigh attached. You see, she was partial to dark meat.

A clean-cut fellow behind the counter, looking fresh out of the laundry in his starched white shirt and his bleached apron, was trying his best not to lose his patience with her. She hunched forward and peered with squinty eyes through the glass display case while he reached his plastic-gloved hand into a pile of chicken parts and held up drumstick-thighs for her inspection. Time and again I watched her scrunch her wizened mouth into a pout and shake her head. "No, son, not that one," she said, or, as he showed her another, "No, that one won't do either." But occasionally she gave a nod, smacked her lips and said, "Yep, now there's a keeper," after which, the attendant gave a not-so-subtle roll of his eyes and set her selection on the scale.

After several minutes of this, the clerk had finally had enough. "Lady, excuse me, but what's wrong with the rest of these hindquarters? All nice and fresh. Why, they're free-range, what more could you want?"

The woman pulled herself back upright and looked him in the eye. "Sure," she said. A little strutting around and exercise would give a chicken some honest taste, indeed. But what she was after, as she'd already mentioned, was some choice dark meat. She could tell at a glance the leg upon which a chicken roosted each night, and that was the one she wanted. "That's the leg where all the flavor goes," she said. "You learn to pay attention, son, and you can tell the difference."

"Well, I'll be," he said, raising his eyebrows. He stood quiet for a moment, then apparently decided it best to humor her, for he shrugged his shoulders and set back to sorting out the rest of her five pounds. He reached for a leg, then glanced at the pile on the scale and his face broadened with a toothy grin. "Ohhh, I get it. All we've got up here is right-sided hindquarters. That must mean chickens always roost on their

right foot. Why didn't you just tell me?" He inspected the piece in his hand, saw it was a left leg,
and tossed it back into the bin before the woman
could stop him.

"Ah, ah, ah. Not so fast, you," she said. "I'll be
wanting that one. That chicken was a lefty."

Of Cabbages and Kings

SAUERKRAUT IS NOT a dish you will find on too many American dinner tables these days. Frankly, it suffers from a frumpy image. Sauerkraut is something that waits limp and forgotten in a cafeteria buffet. Something Opal and Mavis dish up at the Grange for Friday night supper. Definitely not something you'd serve on a first date. Impress your new sweetheart with a platter of thyme-roasted squab on a bed of couscous, by all means, but do not set out a bowl of sauerkraut.

Sauerkraut is not epicurean fare upon which you dine, it is fodder upon which you subsist. Its origins date back to the Chinese, who fed cabbage preserved in wine to workers on the Great Wall. Sauerkraut migrated west in the baggage of the Tartar horsemen; they made it their sustenance when they invaded central Europe. Pliny mentions that the Romans ate cabbages preserved in oil and saltpeter during the winter months. And sauerkraut was partially responsible for Captain James Cook's triumphant second voyage around the world. He insisted it be included on his ship's list of provisions, and its high vitamin C content kept his men from coming down with scurvy.

The word "sauerkraut," which means "sour cabbage," comes from the Germans; the dish had become an integral part of their cuisine by the seventeenth century, as well as a peasant staple in Old World regions from Alsace to Estonia. Long northern winters kept a farmer from growing warm-weather crops like figs and artichokes, but his hearty cabbages could thrive in a short, cool growing season. When his wife preserved the cabbages in salt, she could count on food in the larder to last the winter. And when the farmer's sons and daughters gathered their bags for America, they did not forget how they had feasted like kings and queens on humble cabbage.

When these immigrants arrived, Americans belittled them for their thick accents and tattered clothes, but they welcomed sauerkraut with open arms. The fare of slaves and paupers! It's a wonder they allowed it on their plates, but pile it on they did. Sauerkraut became a mainstay of the frontier. Housewives in South Dakota stored it in the root cellar, in between the crock of pickles and the sack of turnips. And in the city, sauerkraut became a staple of the neighborhood delicatessen. Proprietors in Brooklyn packed it between slices of corned beef and pumpernickel, or tucked it alongside mustard-slapped kielbasa cradled in a bun. Not even the War to End All Wars could snuff the American flame of passion for sauerkraut. The national dish of Germany? Not to worry. They changed its name to Liberty Cabbage and helped themselves to seconds.

This passion for sauerkraut proved to be no more than passing fancy. Food fashions, like hemlines, have always been subject to popular whim; they change at the drop of a kitchen knife. Liberty Cabbage has become passé. We may now eat Pahd Thai and Jamaican jerked sausage, but sauerkraut is no longer in vogue.

This fact I understood all too clearly when I entered the cooking profession. I regarded my own fondness for sauerkraut as a sign of an uneducated palate. I felt it a handicap, indeed, to have been weaned on home cookin' instead of *haute cuisine*. Yet I managed to master the Mother Sauces in the kitchen with ease. I perfected the art of whisking while making *sauce béarnaise*. It's all in the wrist. I made a shallot and vinegar reduction over a high flame, and learned to spot the precise syrupy instant to swirl in the butter so as not to break my *beurre blanc*.

Since I knew I could not really learn to cook until I learned to taste, I took great pains to keep my palate in a rarefied culinary atmosphere. Instead of fried eggs at breakfast, I ate *quiche lorraine*. No milk for me, I drank Perrier. A restaurant hamburger with French fries? How common. Bring me *entrecôte*, grilled rare, please, with a side of *pommes frites*.

But try as I might, I could not elevate my taste buds to the proper *haute* plane. The caviar that we oh-so-sparingly spooned atop poached filet of salmon? To me, it was bait for trout. And the crystal clear pheasant consommé with julienne carrot and leek? I preferred my mother's chicken soup.

It was a hard fact to accept. I did not inherit a silver palate through good breeding, and I could not create one through perseverance. I blame the whole sorry truth on my paternal grandmother's garden.

That garden was not for cultivating a taste in caviar, it was for cultivating cabbages and beans. I look back on it and see dinner still growing in the soil. I understand her garden now as a connection to the land, a source of bounty and synchrony with the seasons. I'll confess that growing up, I didn't always see it that way. I can just about hear my exasperated mother saying, "Would you like me to call your Nana on the phone and tell her you won't eat the carrots she grew in her garden with her own sweat and tears? I didn't think so. Now you clean your plate." Or, at fourteen and miserable, how I wished my dopey mother would just buy her vegetables at the grocery store like everybody else's mom, and quit dragging me out to the farm to help with the weeding.

But after I left home and started cooking for myself, I realized the wealth of fresh flavors I had taken for granted in my grandmother's garden. That garden is why my preferences run toward tender young peas, shelled outdoors in June, eaten raw, two pods for the basket, one for me. It is why I relish the first red potatoes of the season, boiled until their jackets burst, then rolled in melted butter and fresh chopped parsley. And it's why I know how to savor a good, ripe tomato. Not a hothouse, not a hydroponic, but a fat beefsteak, plucked from the vine on an August afternoon, and eaten on the spot, with its sun-warmed juices dribbling down my chin.

And because that garden teemed with cabbages, I have a penchant for what some would call a paltry dish of sauerkraut. One bite of it conjures up vegetable gardens, 100-degree-in-the-shade afternoons, earthenware crocks, and warm soil under bare feet. It also summons up visions of my grandmother, who has put up quite a bit of sauerkraut in her day.

In the sprawling countryside of eastern Washington State where she grew up, making sauerkraut was just what farmwives did, usually after they canned tomatoes and right before they made applesauce. Her tattered loose-leaf notebook bulges with the recipes she has collected during a lifetime of preserving summer harvests. Page after page, she has jotted down recipes in her tidy, schoolgirl script. A few brittle sheets reveal her mother's hand in blotted India ink. Green Tomato Relish, Dilly Beans, Pickled Beets, Piccalilli, Pear Honey, Strawberry-Rhubarb Jam. She never will forgive herself for losing that old recipe for Muzzy's Brandied Fruit Compote. It went to the grave with her mother, rest her soul, and now it's gone for good.

One thing she's not sure she ever had is a recipe for sauerkraut. Heaven knows, she might have a copy stashed away somewhere. No need for one, really. Sauerkraut has just two ingredients: fresh cabbage and salt.

Nana has the ingredients on her mind this late August morning. An entourage of relatives has assembled in her backyard — including my mother, my three sisters and me — and we are ready to make sauerkraut. I'm especially excited this year, because I'm eleven, and that's old enough to grate the cabbage. The cabbages wait in a wheelbarrow by the picnic table. Thirty tight, green heads, cut from the garden before breakfast, already warm from the sun. And it promises to be a hot one. Not yet ten o'clock, but yesterday's roses are dropping their petals, and the meadowlark is done singing until dusk.

A young cousin gives the pile a good sluice with the garden hose. He has been instructed by Nana not to go getting them too clean, though, for it's the good germs on the leaves that make for sauerkraut in the first place. So he soon turns the spray on his brother, who runs squealing across the lawn.

The benevolent germs in question are *Leuconostoc mesenteroids* and *Lactobacillus plantarum*. They have a predilection for saline solutions. A crock of salted cabbage is an immense prairie for them to homestead according to some molecular version of Manifest Destiny. The metabolic product of their toil is an enzyme called lactic acid, which ferments the cabbage and results in the characteristic taste and texture we've come to call sauerkraut.

Nana is no scientist, but she knows a good germ when she tastes it. One by one, we remove the loose outer leaves from each cabbage. With dishtowel, apron corner or shirttail, we wipe from the crisp heads any last traces of soil. We do not call it dirt. Dirt is what sticks underneath your fingernails or behind your ears. But when it plays host to the vegetables you've pulled from your garden, you call it soil.

One aunt halves the cabbages with brisk strokes of her kitchen cleaver, and another carves out the thick cores with a paring knife. Nana shreds the heads into slaw with the kraut-cutter that had been her mama's.

A kraut-cutter is a metal grating contraption. It is an arm's-length long, and the span of an outstretched-hand wide. Kraut-cutters are hard to come by these days, although you can pick one up at a flea market if you're lucky. Nana, who is now eighty-some, has told me I can have hers someday, but she's not finished with it just yet. Kraut-cutters are the instrument of choice when it comes to making sauerkraut, for they quickly turn the cabbage into shreds as thin as quarters, which encourages the osmotic flow of juices that starts the fermentation. A well-honed kitchen knife can do the job, but be careful to cut fine slices, or your cabbage won't juice-up, and it will mold instead of ferment.

We set to grating in Nana's yard. Mother after daughter after aunt after cousin, we spell one another, grating away until our respective old or young arms give out — Hold your hand away from that blade, dear, you'll slice your finger to the bone if you're not careful. Part orchestra, part assembly line, the resonant rap of cleaver on cutting board and the washboard rasp of cabbage against grater keep time.

My mother measures out slaw, five pounds to the batch, on an old grain scale. She dumps it into a metal washtub, throws in three tablespoons of pickling salt, and works it together with her hands, really roughs it up until clear juices stream forth and foam bubbles on the surface. Three or four pairs of young cousins' hands help out, squeezing the cabbage between stubby fingers, and packing it into a ten-gallon earthenware crock. They steal away handfuls of cool,

crisp cabbage, dripping with brine. Gritty undis-
solved crystals stick to small fingers, then melt on
warm tongues. A little one starts to cry, poor dear
has a cut on her thumb. The salty brine stings deep
and Nana says, Come now, honey, nothing a Band-
Aid and a kiss won't mend.

Hard telling if some of us — the grandchildren
— aren't more trouble underfoot than we are help.
Which is perhaps why no one seems to mind when a
few half-pints lose interest and bound off to the corn
rows. The rest of us grate and pack, grate and pack,
into the afternoon. It takes two aunts to haul the
crock off to the cellar, then Nana presses a clean
muslin cloth over the slaw, saturating it in the foamy
brine. On top of the cloth she places a large plate,
then fills a gallon Mason jar with water and sets it
on the plate to weight the sauerkraut down.

Nana wipes her hands on her apron and gives
the crock a hard look. She wrinkles her brow, purses
her lips, and counts on her fingers. "Ten, eleven,
twelve. A dozen batches on the scale. Five pounds to
a batch. That's sixty pounds. A pint's a pound the
world around." She pauses and lifts her eyebrows,
glancing toward my mother, with whom she has a
long-standing argument on this particular axiom.
She is waiting for my mother to point out that a pint
of lead does not equal a pint of feathers in pounds.
But my mother does not take the bait. She knows
the point is moot; the formula works for sauerkraut.

So Nana continues her calculations. "Two pints to a quart. Thirty quarts of 'kraut we've got here." And they leave their good day's work to bubble away quietly in the cellar.

Sauerkraut fermenting underneath a weighted plate requires daily tending. The foam that rises to the top needs a skim, the cloth needs changing, and any hints of mold need to be thoroughly removed. Nana carried out these duties with more faithfulness than most, but with slightly less diligence, perhaps, than the situation warranted. She was just plain too busy, she said, to be perfect. She occasionally found her cabbage darkened with a thin layer of mold, in which case she discarded the affected area, usually the top inch, then she scolded herself under her breath and accepted her losses. As a consequence, Nana allowed herself an expendable cabbage budget. She figured on shredding more cabbage than her family could eat in a year, even the sauerkraut-loving German in-laws she acquired when she married my grandfather. Four to six weeks later, after the bubbling stopped, she had plenty of the translucent, delicious stuff to seal in Ball jars and set on her pantry shelf or pass along to her daughters-in-law.

I have since learned from my county extension agent that you can place a sheet of plastic wrap directly over the cabbage, then fill a large, heavy plastic bag with water and set it on top of the plastic wrap, weighting down the cabbage underneath the brine.

Tie the bag shut with a string and arrange it to form an airtight seal against the sides of the crock, and then you don't have to worry about mold.

I grew up eating sauerkraut throughout the year, cooked with roast pork, heaped on Reuben sandwiches, stirred into baked beans. But if you ask me, the best way to fix it is to start by rendering a few slabs of thick, sliced bacon in a Dutch oven. Pour off the drippings, add a couple of diced onions, a few smashed cloves of garlic, and cook over a low flame until the onions are translucent and the aroma of garlic wafts into the air. Add a quart of sauerkraut — if it's not homemade, rinse it in water to wash away the extra salt — and break up the strands with the tines of a fork. Should the mood strike you, throw in a grated tart apple, a couple of bay leaves, some cracked black pepper, and a dozen or so juniper berries. A dozen red potatoes, halved or quartered, depending on their size, also make a nice addition. Pour in a healthy dose of white wine and a pint of rich chicken stock. Or not; water will suffice. Put a lid on the pot and simmer the sauerkraut until the potatoes just give way to a knife. Check the pot on occasion, and add more liquid if the sauerkraut seems to be drying out.

Now take some smoked link sausages, something along the lines of bratwurst or knockwurst or Polish sausage, and sear them on all sides in a little oil in a hot skillet — plan on two links per person.

Add the links to the sauerkraut and let the kettle simmer for another half hour. Take the meal to the table and serve it with coarse brown mustard and a heavy round of sourdough rye.

Dish up the sauerkraut and breathe deep the pine scent of juniper, the apple-wood smoke of sausage. Slather mustard on the potatoes and the links, and sop up the juices with hunks torn from the loaf of bread. Wash it down with a glass of dry Riesling or long pulls from a bottle of dark ale. Try to remember as you eat that sauerkraut is not ambrosia of the gods and it is not the latest rage. It is the swill of serfs and farmhands, who sure knew how to dine.

The Same Old Stuffing

BEFORE YOU SET OUT to revamp your Thanksgiving meal, it pays to consider all the repercussions. Just because the editors of the glossy food magazines have grown weary of the same old turkey and fixings, and even though they are absolutely giddy with excitement over the smoked quail, the spicy black bean stuffing, and the sun-dried tomato and arugula gratin they have in store for this year's feast, it does not mean that everyone will welcome innovation at the Thanksgiving table. Quite the contrary. All some people really want is the tried and true. Some people have grown quite fond of their annual mix of turkey and trimmings, each and every dish, and they do not consider it an onerous task to repeat the meal from one year to the next. They gain comfort from the familiarity and the ritual of it all; any tampering with the menu, no matter how minor or well intentioned, only serves to make them feel shortchanged.

This fact my mother discovered to her dismay when she tried out a little something at our own Thanksgiving meal. For years before anyone realized it had become a tradition, she roasted our holiday turkey with two types of stuffing inside it. She filled the bird's main cavity with my paternal grandmother's sage-and-onion dressing. This quintessential American farmhouse preparation was a genuine family heirloom, as Nana had learned to make it at her own mother's side. And for the bird's neck cavity, my mom fixed what you could call an Italian-American hybrid stuffing. Although this filling was not authentically Italian, it was a recipe from my mother's family, and it bespoke her immigrant heritage with its classic Mediterranean combination of sausage, spinach, raisins and nuts.

Then one autumn as the holiday loomed near, my mom found herself contemplating our annual Thanksgiving spread. She saw it suddenly in a new and somewhat bothersome light. What had seemed a skillful act of diplomacy all these years, this bringing together of two family traditions inside one bird, why, it now smacked to her of excess. How the fact had escaped her for so long, she did not know, for she did not go for over-indulgence when it came to family meals. My mother was accommodating, don't misunderstand me. She was a mom who once finished up a marathon session of Dr. Seuss books with a breakfast of green eggs and ham at the behest of her four daughters. Still, she made us eat our peas, and she said things like, "The day your papa starts raising cows that don't come with livers is the day I'll quit serving liver and onions for dinner. Now eat up." Yes, she knew where to draw the line.

What suddenly struck my mother as disturbing was not a matter of gluttony or expense or grams of fat, but of balance. What with the mashed potatoes, the baked yams, the penny rolls, and two types of stuffing, there was altogether too much starch on the plate. Starch, starch, starch. The redundancy of it became an offense that the English teacher in her could no longer abide. Of an instant, the solution became clear: two stuffings were one stuffing too many. One of them would have to go.

So she said to my father, "Jim, which stuffing do you prefer at Thanksgiving?"

He replied, "My mother's sage-and-onion dressing, of course. It's the stuffing of my youth. It's the heart of the Thanksgiving meal. By God, it's a national tradition, that stuffing, and I can't even imagine the holiday without it."

This was not the response my mother had in mind. Nana's sage-and-onion dressing had been her candidate for dismissal, because naturally, she preferred her family's stuffing, the one with the Italian touch of sausage, spinach and raisins. She saw my father's point, though. We celebrated the holiday with his side of the family, and she had them to bear in mind. The children would be too preoccupied with the mashed potatoes to care a whit one way or the other about the stuffing, but her in-laws would feel deprived, no doubt, if Nana's dish didn't grace the table. And she had to admit that the sage-and-onion version was more in keeping with the all-American spirit of the holiday. It was more faithful, she assumed, to history. Good heavens, even schoolchildren knew that sage-and-onion dressing appeared on the Pilgrims' rough-hewn banquet table, right alongside the spit-roasted wild turkey, the hearth-braised sweet potatoes, the cranberry sauce, and the pumpkin pie.

I must admit I envisioned such a meal, just as I pictured Miles Standish brandishing a kitchen knife and gallantly carving the turkey roast while he gazed deep into the limpid eyes of Priscilla Mullens. But there is no record of stuffing — sage-and-onion or otherwise — bedecking the table at the Pilgrims' first thanksgiving, which it turns out was not a somber meal, but a frolicsome affair of hunting, games, and wine which lasted three days. For that matter, there isn't even any specific mention of turkeys having been served, though one colonist wrote of an abundance of fowl at the event, and most scholars feel safe in assuming this bounty included a few turkeys. All anyone knows for certain is that the Mayflower folks cooked up five deer, oysters, cod, eel, corn bread, goose, watercress, leeks, berries, and plums. Pumpkins made an appearance, too, but no one bothered to record just how they were cooked. They certainly were not baked in a pie crust, though, for the wheat crop had failed and the ship's supply of flour had long since run out.

The traditional meal as we know it dates back not to the solemn, high-collared Pilgrims, nor even to Colonial times, but to home cooks of the nineteenth century. Not until this era did the idea of an annual day of thanksgiving first take hold. The driving force behind the holiday was New Englander Sarah Josepha Hale (whose legacy also includes the nursery rhyme "Mary Had a Little Lamb"). As editor of the popular magazine *Godey's Lady's Book*, she promoted the holiday for nearly twenty years within the periodical's pages. She wrote letters annually to the state governors and to the president, and one by one the states gradually took up the idea. Finally, Abraham Lincoln, desperate for any means to promote unity in the war-ravaged country, declared the first national Thanksgiving in 1863.

And what did the mistress of the house serve up at this new holiday meal? Her standard company fare for autumn, of course: roast turkey with cranberry sauce, scalloped and mashed potatoes, candied sweet potatoes, braised turnips, creamed onions, cranberry sauce, mince pie, pumpkin pie — the menu has endured remarkably unchanged. And yes, it was standard procedure then to roast the turkey with a stuffing.

The actual practice of filling up a bird's cavity dates back to antiquity; the space made a handy cooking vessel for families who all too often owned only one pot. Recipes have varied over the millennia. The cookbook attributed to the Roman gastronome Apicius gives a formula that includes ground meat, chopped brains, couscous, pine nuts, lovage, and ginger; other than the brains, it sounds like something right out of a trendy contemporary cookbook. English cooks during the Middle Ages favored heavily spiced and honeyed productions based on pieces of offal that today would make our rarefied stomachs churn. Nineteenth-century American cooks went on stuffing birds, no matter how many pots and pans they had on hand in the kitchen, and recipes much like Nana's sage-and-onion dressing were a beloved part of many an early Thanksgiving repast.

No less dear, though, or popular, or traditional, were a number of other variations. Homemakers in the corn-growing south who went to stuff a turkey favored cornbread in their recipes. Along the eastern seaboard, they tucked in dozens of nectar-sweet shucked oysters, while across the country as far north as the chestnut tree once grew, they featured loads of tender chestnuts in their fillings. And many cooks treasured recipes that called for ground meat, dried fruits, autumn greens, and shelled nuts — the very products of the fall harvest upon which my mother's family recipe was based, so she need not have dismissed her version as unconventional so hastily.

The genteel ladies of the last century would have viewed my mother's dilemma not as a surplus of starch at the meal, but as a paucity of meats. They were impassioned carnivores, these American predecessors of ours, and one meager turkey would have seemed woefully inadequate at a meal showcasing the prodigious bounty of the land. Pull out the stops, Darlene, I can all but hear them tell her. Along with the requisite turkey, they decorated their tables with a chicken pie, a joint of beef, a roast goose, if the budget would allow. Certainly these additional viands would serve to put my mother's menu back on kilter.

I'm sure, too, that at least one of these women would have felt bound by duty to draw my mother aside and whisper that she really ought to call her preparation *dressing* and not *stuffing*. The word "stuffing" has been in use for centuries. Sir Thomas Elyot's *Dictionary* of 1538 uses it as a synonym for "forcemeat," defined as "that wherewith any foule is crammed." Sir Thomas obviously wasn't much of a cook, or he would have known that cramming a fowl isn't such a great idea, for the filling expands during the roasting, and it can burst out at the seams if it is packed too tightly. At any rate, all this stuffing and forcing and cramming proved simply too much for the delicate sensibilities of the Victorian age, and the more discreet term "dressing" came into fashion. Today, schoolmarmish cookbooks often wag a finger and insist that when it is on the inside of the bird it is stuffing, and when it is baked in a separate dish, it's dressing. In reality, this does not play out. If Grandma calls her dish stuffing, then stuffing it is, regardless of its location inside or alongside the bird. Same goes for Aunt Pearl's dressing, no matter where she puts it.

Had my mother sought the counsel of Mrs. Sarah Josepha Hale or her contemporaries, then, she might have spared herself some anxiety. For although she had resolved herself to her decision, the idea of forgoing her family recipe did not rest easy with her. The days wore on and she grew positively disgruntled. Then one brisk, gray morning with two weeks yet to go before Thanksgiving, she found herself pushing her cart down the butcher's aisle at the supermarket when inspiration struck. Who ever said holiday recipes were for holidays, and holidays only? Who? She need not go without her annual dose of her family's stuffing after all. So she hoisted a fresh turkey into the cart, made a few other spur-of-the-moment additions to her shopping list, and went home and set to work.

She pulled her big frying pan out of the cupboard, set it over a low flame on the stove-top, melted half a stick of butter in it, then crumbled in three-quarters of a pound of bulk pork sausage. After the meat began to brown, she stirred in a diced onion, a couple of cloves of pressed garlic, a few stalks of cut-up celery, and a cup or so of sliced button mushrooms. These she let simmer gently until the onions were translucent. She added a large container of the chopped garden spinach she had blanched and frozen last spring, heated it through, then scraped the contents of the pan into a large ceramic bowl. When the mixture cooled to room temperature she sliced a stale loaf of French bread into cubes — enough to make about four cups — then added the bread to the bowl along with a couple of ample handfuls of raisins, sliced almonds, and freshly grated Parmesan cheese — a good half cup of each. She seasoned the stuffing with salt, black pepper, and generous pinches of oregano and rosemary, then drizzled in a glass of white wine. Using her hands, she combined all the ingredients thoroughly, then put a finger to her tongue. A pinch more salt and that would do it. Finally, she spooned the stuffing into the bird, trussed it up, and put it in the oven to roast for the rest of the afternoon.

Incidentally, my mother is quite an accomplished seamstress. She could sew bound buttonholes on a turkey if she wanted to. But she agrees with me that trussing need not be the intricate knit-one-purl-two operation that many cookbooks describe. Such elaborate needlework lingers from the days of the kitchen hearth-fire, when trussing was done to keep the drumsticks and wings from dangling in the flames as the bird turned on a spit. It now functions as a stuffy, old guard test of a cook's dexterity — yes, but can she truss a turkey? By the turn of this century, the massive iron kitchen range had become a standard feature in the American home, and oven roasting rendered unnecessary all the knotting and stitching and battening down. Trussing now primarily serves to keep the stuffing in place, and to give the bird a demure appearance, its ankles politely crossed, when it arrives at the table. Folding back the wings and tying the drumsticks together with kitchen twine usually make for ample treatment.

As my mom put the neck and giblets into a stock-pot on the stove for gravy, she decided a side dish of mashed potatoes would be just the accompaniment to round out the meal. Then she discovered she had a few sweet potatoes in the bin under the kitchen sink, and she thought, now wouldn't those be nice, too, roasted with a little butter, ginger, and brown sugar? And when she remembered the tiny boiling onions that had been rolling around in the refrigerator's bottom drawer, she decided she might as well bake them up au gratin with some bread crumbs and cream.

The turkey spittered and spattered away in the oven, filling every nook in the house with its buttery, winter-holiday scent, and the next thing my mom knew, she was rolling out the crust for a pumpkin pie. My father arrived home from work, draped his overcoat across the banister, and walked into the kitchen just in time to see her plopping the cranberry sauce out of the can. She placed it on the table in a sterling silver dish, its ridged imprints still intact and its jellied body quivering gloriously — God bless those folks at Ocean Spray, they were always a part of our turkey dinners, too. She turned to my father and said, "Dinner's almost ready."

My mom watched as her family gathered around the table and enjoyed a complete turkey feast on that evening in early November. After the meal, my father stretched back in his chair and folded his hands behind his head. He'd always thought it a shame, he said, a needless deprivation, that Americans ate roast turkey only once a year at Thanksgiving. This fine dinner just proved his point. What a treat, yes, what a treat. But the family's pleasure that night was merely an added perk for my mother, as she had prepared the meal for herself, only for herself, and she was feeling deeply satisfied.

When the official holiday finally arrived, my mother made good on her vow and let Nana's sage-and-onion dressing preside at the evening meal. Out came the frying pan, and she started to sauté two chopped onions and four thinly sliced stalks of celery, including the leaves, in a stick of butter. After a moment's thought, she added two plump cloves of minced garlic to the simmering pan. She couldn't resist. She knew Nana thought her a bit heavy-handed in the garlic department, but so what, it was her kitchen.

When the vegetables were limp and fragrant, she pulled the pan from the heat and set it aside to cool. She put the mixture into a bowl along with eight cups of firm, stale bread cubes, a generous spoonful of dried sage, a healthy handful of chopped fresh parsley, some salt and pepper, and a pinch of nutmeg. She gave these ingredients a light mixing, drizzled in enough broth to make the filling hold together when she squeezed a handful of it between her fingers — three-quarters of a cup, maybe a bit more — then tossed the dressing together again lightly before she spooned it into the Thanksgiving bird.

That evening Nana arrived with her sweet pickles and her three pies — apple, pumpkin, mincemeat. Cousins poured into the house toting covered casserole dishes, an uncle walked through the door, then an aunt. We soon sat down around two tables to dine, our plates heaped to the angle of repose. Amid the clanking of cutlery and the giggling and guffawing, and the festive bustle, my father paused. His fork pierced a juicy slice of dark thigh meat and his knife was poised in midstroke. He looked down intently and his eyes circled clockwise, studying the contents of his plate. He craned his neck and took an inventory of the platters and bowls laid out on the buffet counter across the room. "Darlene," he said, "this is some spread we have here, don't get me wrong. But you know what's missing is that other stuffing you make. The one we had the other day with the cornucopia of raisins and nuts and such."

My mom nearly dropped her fork. "But you told me you preferred your mother's dressing."

He looked back down at the turkey and trimmings before him. "Well, yes, but that doesn't mean I don't prefer yours, too. It just doesn't seem like a proper Thanksgiving without that second stuffing on the table. Don't you agree?"

What he meant, of course, was that my mom's dish had to turn up missing before he understood just what a part of the celebration it had become. So the year the turkey had only one stuffing was the year that both recipes became permanent fixtures on my mother's Thanksgiving menu. When time-honored traditions get their start while you're not looking, it seems, they need not concern themselves with balance, or daily nutritional requirements, or even historical accuracy. For such rituals rise up out of memories, and memories are not subject to hard facts. They are not interested in making room for change.

When Fathers Cook

IF ANYONE HAD ASKED me when I was a child, I would have said that fathers could cook only fried eggs, hash browned potatoes, and barbecued steaks. And peanut butter cookies, big ones. But that's it. Fathers came home from work in the evening, loosened their ties, and read the paper. Mothers cooked. Not for fathers the drudgery of meat loaves and casseroles, or the banality of domestic economy. Even when I was ten, and my father got it into his head to enroll in an evening culinary arts course for men, I would not have called what he did in the kitchen "cooking." He made no pot pies, no dumplings with pan gravy, no jam. Indeed, he did not don apron and pick up cleaver in the kitchen merely to cook, he came to perform.

My father followed in the tradition of the great professional chefs of Europe: men who knew the dining table as theater; who busied themselves flambéing tournedos and codifying their formalized repertoire of *haute cuisine*. These chefs did not bother with uncomplicated stews or slow-simmered chickens in pots. Such common fare they dismissed as *la cuisine des femmes:* rustic dishes cooked by peasant women with the ingredients at hand and made from unwritten recipes passed down through the generations. *Cuisine des femmes?* the upper culinary ranks were wont to exclaim, why that's what wives stirred up to stick to the ribs of their trenchermen husbands, and it's what mothers cooked to quiet the empty stomachs of their ragamuffin broods. No matter that many a culinary great earned his Michelin stars by showcasing dishes that his own mother used to make.

For six consecutive Tuesdays my father set out to study the principles of *escalopes de veau gratinées, coquilles Saint-Jacques,* and *sauce hollandaise.* His culinary skills blossomed under the exacting tutelage of his course instructor, Chef Bradley, who had sautéed and whisked cover to cover through both volumes of *Mastering the Art of French Cooking.* And we, his family, were the beneficiaries of his growing expertise.

One afternoon a few weeks after he finished his course, my father arrived home early from his law office with his arms loaded down with groceries. He

announced there would be no need for the lasagna
my mother had prepared for dinner that night.
Indeed, it could wait until tomorrow. He kissed my
mother on the cheek, patted her on the elbow, and
told her to go on upstairs and draw herself a nice,
relaxing bath. No, he assured her, he didn't need
help with a thing. He had his recipe. He had his
notes. And tonight for the delight of his wife and
four daughters, he would make — cioppino!

Cioppino is a hearty fish stew, redolent of garlic
and tomatoes and the brine of the sea. A specialty of
the early immigrants along Fisherman's Wharf in
San Francisco, the dish is of uncertain parentage,
and there are countless tales of its origin. Some say
cioppino is the legacy of the Portuguese who settled
on the shores of California. Others maintain the
stew came from the Italians who inhabited San
Francisco's North Beach — in some now-forgotten
dialect "cioppino" means "to chop up," which
Italian housewives did to the fish before adding
them to their spicy broth. Or, as one story claims,
the name came from a motley group of failed immigrant prospectors after the gold rush of 1849. These
haggard men hung around the dockyards and
begged for handouts from the fishermen. "Chip in!
Chip in!" they cried in their thick accents, and they
cooked their gleanings in a communal kettle over an
open fire, sopping up the juices with thick hunks of
their sourdough bread.

Regardless of origin, cioppino has fallen prey to its own popularity in recent years. Corner-cutting, insensitive restaurateurs have all but reduced it to a steam-table galley slave. They serve it underseasoned and overboiled in portions undersized and overpriced. But a far greater tragedy, an employer of mine once lamented, is that bouillabaisse has met a similar fate. You see, she explained, bouillabaisse, that elegant culinary gem of Marseilles, is the standard by which all seafood stews are measured, and cioppino is but its tawdry cousin. Perhaps I should have reminded her that most Mediterranean-inspired seafood stews originated as messy, put-on-a-bib-and-eat-with-your-fingers affairs. With their bones and shells and dribbling juices they were not meant for the prim of heart or the clean of finger. From cioppino all the way to bouillabaisse, they evolved as a hearty means of using up trash fish — the odds and ends and uglies that didn't sell at the market that day. While these dishes may differ in geography and technique, they share a common spirit, for they pay tribute to a long line of cooks who knew how to make something out of nothing.

You might be wondering why my father, whose hands had partaken in the making of *tournedos sautés chasseur* and *bavarois à la vanille,* would concern himself with the likes of such a dish. Bear in mind that during the seventies in the landlocked Yakima Valley of Washington, fish were white-fleshed and frozen. They came from the supermarket in plastic-wrapped Styrofoam, and, like company, they were good in the home for three days before they started to smell. So cioppino, with its fresh ocean riches, was exotic fare indeed.

As for my mother, who was she to refuse such a generous offer? She took a quick look at his recipe, brought a quart jar of her tomatoes up from the cellar pantry, pulled a Tupperware of stock from the freezer, and then repaired to the bath.

Such a feast called for a good measure of drama. Clearly some background music was in order, said my father as we, his daughters, gathered around to take in the show. Something festive. Something with enough flair to befit the occasion. "No, girls, not 'Someone's in the Kitchen with Dinah.' We are not going to sing along with Mitch Miller, I don't care what your mom lets you listen to." He went to the stereo cabinet and thumbed through his record collection. "Ah, just the ticket," he said, blowing the dust from the album. "This will get us in the mood." And he rolled up his shirtsleeves and set to work, humming along with Beethoven, *allegro ma non troppo,* the opening notes of Symphony Number Nine.

Perhaps if my father had enrolled in one of Chef Bradley's advanced culinary courses, or if he had paid a touch more attention to my mother in the kitchen, he would have had a vague notion of what the French call *mise en place.* Roughly translated, and in the words of Mary Poppins, this phrase means "a place for everything and everything in its place." Before any actual stove-work begins, the experienced cook reads through a recipe, assembles at close range all the necessary utensils, and has all the ingredients cleaned, chopped, and ready for the pot.

In lieu of experience and his *mise en place*, my father had confidence, so he tied on his barbecuing apron and took it from the top. Of the recipe, that is, and worked his way to the bottom. "Clean, cook, and crack two large Dungeness crabs," his recipe read. That was easy; the good gentleman at the fish market had done it for him. In the West, Dungeness crabs are perhaps the quintessential ingredient in cioppino. Named for the five-mile Dungeness sand spit on Washington State's Olympic Peninsula, they can be found along the Pacific coast from central California to the Aleutians and in most seafood delicatessens in between. Although purists may find the practice heretical, declared my father's recipe, Alaska king crab, Maine lobster, or even a pound of sea scallops would suffice in a pinch.

Because my father had watched Chef Bradley prepare *velouté de crévette*s, and *moules à la mariniére,* he had no problem peeling and deveining his pound of medium shrimp or scrubbing and bearding his pound of mussels. And he figured the pound of steamer clams he purchased could use a good scrubbing as well. He ran the tip of a paring knife down to the fourth line in his recipe. "Cut one pound of red snapper or other firm-fleshed fish into two-inch pieces," he read aloud. "This cooking business is such a cakewalk, really," he said as he sliced up the lingcod that the salesclerk had recommended.

He turned his attention to dicing a large onion, then took out his whetstone. "How in the world your mom manages to get a thing done in this kitchen with her dull knives, I'll never know," he muttered. He touched the blade with the nail of his thumb, pronounced its edge much better, and set a blistering pace as he thinly sliced two stalks of celery and diced one green and one red bell pepper. But he lost his stride when he turned the page and his recipe called for four large cloves of minced garlic. Chef Bradley had a special gadget that you put a clove into, squeezed, and out came minced garlic. He rummaged through my mother's utensil drawer and came up empty-handed. How could he proceed without one? He wiped his hands dry on a kitchen towel and mopped the perspiration that had arisen along his receding hairline. Then he headed up the stairs, bulb of garlic in hand, and flung open the bathroom door. "How am I supposed to squish this?"

My mother laid her *Better Homes and Gardens* magazine on the edge of the tub and looked up at the head of garlic in astonishment. She'd actually grown accustomed to my father's culinary questions of late, although she did not normally field them from the bath. But my mom, who grew up the daughter of Italian immigrants and had been all but weaned on garlic, who had been peeling and mincing garlic cloves since she could reach the counter-top, simply could not fathom why the process needed any explaining in the first place. She sighed. "Pull apart the cloves you need —"

My dad wrestled with the bulb. "Would you consider this a big clove or a medium-sized clove?"

"Medium."

"Oh, dear. My recipe calls for four large."

"Use six of those. You'll be fine," she assured him. "Give them a pop on the cutting board with the flat side of your knife, peel off the papery skin, and then just smash them up. Use the flat side of your knife for that, too."

"Thanks, honey."

After a few minutes my father surveyed his handiwork. Chef Bradley would have been proud. My dad checked his instructions, set a five-quart Dutch oven on the stove-top, then rubbed his hands together briskly. He studied the front of my mother's olive oil tin, and as he poured a quarter cup into the kettle, he wondered just precisely how one went about becoming an extra-virgin.

The answer has nothing to do with vestal priestesses or holy sacraments. Rather, "extra-virgin" refers to oil from the first pressing of the olives, the unctuous, flavorful juices obtained solely through the mechanical crushing of the un-pitted fruit. This "virgin" oil is then graded according to its oleic acid content, a fatty acid that forms when the fat molecules break down. The lower the acidity, the higher the quality of the oil. "Extra-virgin" oil contains less than one percent oleic acid, followed by "superfine-virgin," "fine-virgin," and "virgin," with no more than 1.5, 3, and 4 percent oleic acid, respectively. Subsequent pressings require the use of heat and chemicals to extract additional oil from the olives. The resulting product, harsher and less flavorful than that of the first pressing, is smoothed out with virgin oil and labeled as "pure" because it contains only oil from olives and not from say, corn or grape-seed.

My father heated the oil over a medium flame, and when it started to shimmer, he added the onion, garlic, celery, and bell peppers. He gave the pot a stir, reduced the heat, and let the vegetables sauté gently for a few minutes while he searched the cupboard for the seasonings he needed. He found my mother's stash of Spanish saffron in a Sucret's cough lozenge tin. Had he known that saffron threads are the dried stigmata of *Crocus sativus,* the autumn-flowering crocus, or that field workers must hand-harvest seventy thousand flowers to obtain a pound of these stigmata, or that unadulterated saffron fetches $4500 a pound on the market, he would not have brushed onto the floor the threads he spilled when he went to add a pinch to his simmering pot.

He spotted a canister of thyme leaves, measured out a carefully leveled teaspoon, and sprinkled it over his stew. Next he put in a bay leaf and a half teaspoon of red pepper flakes. He rummaged through the cupboard and came across a jigger full of thumbtacks, a chipped bone china teacup full of bacon grease, an envelope stuffed with Betty Crocker coupons, and a blue jar of Vick's VapoRub that contained the sweet William seeds my mother intended to plant as soon as she remembered where the devil she'd ever put them. But he did not find the next ingredient on his list.

A moment later my mother heard light footsteps on the stairs. She looked up from her magazine as the bathroom door opened, and she saw my sister's grinning, seven-year-old, freckled face peering around from behind it. "Daddy wants to know, what's oh-ray-GONE-oh, and where do you keep it?"

My mom suppressed a smile, gave her an answer, and resumed reading about perennial beds in the new western landscape. With a flip of her ponytail and a "Thanks, Mama," my sister trotted dutifully back down the stairs to the kitchen. "She says it's oh-RAY-gun-oh, and it's in the spice rack."

My father found the oregano jar and added a teaspoon to the pot. Next came red wine. On the recommendation of Chef Bradley, my dad had purchased Sebastiani Cabernet Sauvignon for cooking; a wine economical and readily available, yet still highly palatable. He added a cup to the cioppino, then poured himself a glass and took a sip. Not bad for jug wine.

As the wine bubbled and sputtered in the kettle, my dad picked up my mother's Mason jar of tomatoes and consulted his recipe. He flipped through his notes, then bounded up the stairs two at a time and burst into the bathroom. Did my mother realize that twenty-eight ounces of canned tomatoes were due in his pot in less than three minutes? "How many ounces in this thing?"

"Thirty-two."

"I need twenty-eight. What should I do without a scale, for chrissake?"

"Use the whole jar. It's close enough." Her voice sounded calm, but tired.

"You're sure?"

"Positive. Close the door, will you please, you're letting all the cold air in."

"Sorry, dear."

He made it back to the stove with thirty seconds to spare, added two tablespoons of tomato paste to the vegetables, then poured in the whole jar of tomatoes and crushed them up with a wooden spoon. He pushed his black horn-rimmed glasses back onto the bridge of his nose with a tomato-blotched finger. All he needed now was three cups of fish stock, which he could have made easily by simmering for thirty minutes the shrimp shells and some fish trimmings in water and a little white wine. He could have made it an especially fine stock by adding an onion, a carrot, a stalk of celery, a parsley sprig, and a few pepper-corns. Instead, he eyed the Tupperware on the counter, which my mother had labeled only, "stock." His recipe did mention in parentheses that canned chicken broth or bottled clam nectar diluted with water would make acceptable substitutes for the fish stock. So he grabbed the container, took a deep breath, and up the stairs he trudged.

"What's this?"

My mom let her magazine drop to the floor. Her jaw took on a clenched edge of lost patience, but my father didn't notice. "That?" she said slowly. "That is chicken stock. Some people call it broth. I make it by boiling the carcass after we have roast chicken."

"But my recipe calls for *canned* chicken broth. Chef Bradley only uses Swanson's."

"Well," she said, pulling the plug on the bathtub drain, "How do you think Mrs. Swanson makes her chicken stock?"

"Oh," he replied blankly. He handed her a towel and then returned to the kitchen to add her stock to the pot.

As his stew bubbled softly on the stove top we helped him set the table. Off with these plastic place-mats and out with the lace tablecloth, he instructed us. Uh, Daddy, we told him, the knife and spoon go on the right.

In thirty minutes his rich broth had thickened slightly and even my mother could smell its bold aroma from the bedroom upstairs. After a holler up the stairs, my dad learned that the fresh basil and parsley were growing outside the back door, next to the chrysanthemums. He chopped up a quarter cup of each, stirred them into the stew, checked the seasoning and added some salt, then wiped his hands on the front of his apron. The time had come for the final installment: the adding of the shellfish. He hovered over the stove, recipe in hand, and dropped in the clams and the pieces of crab. He waited while his stew simmered, covered, for about four minutes. "Light the candles!" he shouted. "Somebody go get Mom! We're five minutes away from dinner time!" He added the rest of the shellfish and the lingcod, put the lid back on the kettle, and let everything continue to simmer softly, giving the pot an occasional shake, until the clams and mussels opened, the shrimp turned pink, and the fish had just cooked through.

My mother came down the stairs, all dried and talcum powdered, and wearing a fresh cotton dress for the event. "Well, doesn't that look delicious!" she said as my dad brought the kettle to the table. She really meant it. That pot of cioppino was a thing of beauty to behold. My father ladled it into bowls for all of us, and with the gusto of immigrant fishermen we slurped away from big spoons and pulled apart shellfish with sticky fingers. We slopped spicy, tomato-red broth on my mom's lace tablecloth, and we swabbed the bottoms of our bowls with thick slices of sourdough bread. My father served us out a second round, and my mother dabbed the corners of her mouth with her linen napkin. "You know, girls," she said, "I might have had my doubts, but your father's turning out to be quite a cook."

Yesterday's Bread

YOU CAN MAKE A LOAF of bread with nothing more than flour, water, a cake of yeast, and time. Given enough time, you can even dispense with the yeast-cake, for a hodgepodge of wild yeasts in the air will light on the dough, feed on the flour, and eventually muster enough vigor to make the dough rise. This was the primordial leaven, happened upon some six thousand years ago, historians speculate, when Egyptian slaves left a mix of ground meal and water too long under the warm sun, then found the resulting bread to be soft and airy and eminently more pleasing than the brittle wafers they had set out to make.

Still, to coax life into a shaggy mass of flour, water, and yeast, to turn an unwieldy lump of dough into an auburn-crusted loaf of bread, requires the nurture and guidance of human hands. Even professional artisanal bakers, who knead their doughs in sixty-quart mixers, still insist on rolling and shaping each loaf by hand. Indeed, it is this flour-dusted contact with the baker that makes a hand-crafted loaf one of the most fundamental pleasures of the table, a gift that not only satiates a hungry stomach, but delights the senses. That ingredients so elemental and humble could metamorphose into something so grand is no doubt why the mere thought of producing a loaf of bread fills the fledgling baker with trepidation. It vexes countless home cooks, who have tried and failed, yet still have their sights set on becoming accomplished bakers, lest they suffer the fate of a life with only store-bought bread.

A sharp sales associate at a well-stocked kitchenware shop wouldn't hesitate to point out that these aspiring bakers could solve all their troubles with a bread machine. Why, a bread machine can do the job in a cinch, and without so much as a trace of flour ever smudging the hands. My own attitude toward these machines is not so enthusiastic. I will grant that they do fill a niche. The loaves they produce are leaps and bounds above the squishy fluff that industrial bakers hastily shove into plastic bags. It's not the odd square shape of these loaves that puts me off, it's their insides, the part many bakers call the crumb or the flesh, for want of a better term. The French, who categorically spend more time pondering their food than we do, have a name for the insides of bread. They call it *mie*. They even have *pan de mie*, bread baked in special covered tins that ends up with all insides and no crust. That we make do without such a word as *mie* in English is perhaps indicative of our long-standing indifference to the subject of bread. At any rate, the interior of bread-machine breads has a processed look and feel and taste to it that, while not highly objectionable, fails to win me over. These loaves may be convenient, but as for flavor and aesthetics, the handmade loaf has yet to be eclipsed.

I have a white-haired auntie in Washington who claims that what these frustrated bakers are lacking, the poor dears, is a quality she calls The Touch. No getting around it, she said to me once, her arms plunged deep in her bread bowl, when it comes to baking bread, you have to have The Touch. What Lena has in mind, I've decided, is the mix of sureness and passion and common sense that imbues a loaf of bread with character and dimension. I have felt traces of this Touch in my own hands as I knead my doughs, and the bakers I most admire all seem to possess it, an elusive something that manifests itself in the deep flavor and rustic appearance of their breads. This Touch of Lena's is what distinguishes a well-crafted loaf from all the failed attempts that ended up leaden or gummy or burnt; it is what gives good bread a soul.

Lena is actually my father's aunt. She has lived all her life in the grain-growing country of the Palouse, and she would never call herself a gourmet. She does not make flambéed omelets for instance or *poularde à la parisienne*. But can she ever cook. Just give her a room full of hungry farmers, she told me, and she can cook. Pork chops. Pot roast. Pan gravy. And she is not too humble to admit that bread-baking is her specialty. She makes magnificent farmhouse loaves. Immense, split-topped rounds that rise up in the oven and billow over the sides of their pans like a fat lady in a corset. She has been turning out loaves of bread for seventy years, ever since she was a tiddly snippet, ten years old. Too short to reach the tabletop, she knelt on the pine floor of the family's Endicott homestead and kneaded her dough in a wooden bucket perched on a stool. She could tell, just by opening the oven door and holding her smooth little hand in the airspace, when the wood-fired cookstove was hot enough to take her loaves.

Lena does not believe a body just up and inherits The Touch, even though her mother could bake bread, and she can bake bread, and her sixty-year-old son with his massive, leathery hands, why he can bake bread, too. No, a body, and anybody, at that, comes by The Touch with practice. With patience. Certainly, practice taught her the blood-warm feel of the water she needed to grow her yeast best, a temperature she recognized from dressing barnyard chickens and the pheasants her father brought in from the wheat fields. It was practice that acquainted her with the satiny texture of a well-kneaded piece of dough — soft as a baby's bottom, supple as the lobe of her ear. And only through practice did she learn to pull a loaf of bread from the oven, rap it with her knuckles, and discern by feel and its resonant thump that it was baked through.

A few years ago, Lena took out her manual typewriter with its worn ribbon and its cursive font and tapped out a stack of her recipes. As I sifted through them the other day — streusel bread, raised doughnuts, sour cream twists — I became infused with yeast-scented memories of her. I saw her of an autumn morning, looking out the window at ominous, black clouds, then pronouncing it not an errand-running day, but a bread-baking day, as she pulled out her enormous pine kneading board. I recalled holding a still-warm heel of her bread in the cup of my hand and watching a pat of butter melt into its pores. And I heard again the disappointment in her voice after she fell and sprained her wrist, then reluctantly had to admit she couldn't knead her dough with just one hand.

At the bottom of Lena's stack, I came upon one of my favorites, a recipe for rye bread. Lena says it belonged to my great-grandmother, a woman with big forearms and a tight bun whom I know only from a crumpled photo in my father's footlocker, but who, Lena assures me, was a crackerjack baker in her own right. The recipe does not make the dark, deli-style loaves that many people envision when they think of rye bread. Instead, it yields light loaves with a subtle, nutty tang and just enough rye flavor to evoke our shared Volga-German heritage. It also calls upon the traditions of the farmwives of yesterday, who baked bread, and nicely, with little more than intuition and the warmth of their hands.

As I thought of Lena setting to work on this bread, I realized nothing could ever substitute completely for all the hours and days that have honed her Touch. But it dawned on me that a few glimmers of insight, some explanations as to the mechanisms that give rise to a loaf of bread — well, they couldn't help but take some of the fluster and jitters out of learning to bake.

My mind saw Lena starting in after dinner, with the dishes done and the counters wiped, by boiling a potato — a smallish one, the size of a child's fist — in a pot of water until it could be pierced easily with a knife. When the pot cooled to baby-bottle warm, she peeled and mashed the potato in her heavy bread bowl, then poured one and a half cups of the cooking liquid in on top of it. She dissolved a teaspoon of yeast in a half cup of warm water, waited a few minutes for it to froth, and drizzled this mixture into the bowl. Next, she stirred in a cup each of white and rye flour, then covered the bowl with a towel and left it in a draft-free place until morning.

This gloppy paste is called a sponge, and it is a vestige of the days before commercial yeast. Yeasts are microscopic fungi that have proved themselves most useful over the millennia. They are ubiquitous, but because they like sweet, moist places, they tend to congregate on the skins of fruit, on flowers rich with nectar, and on kernels of grain. There, they feast on sugars, producing alcohol and carbon dioxide. They turn grape pressings into wine, apple pressings into hard cider, honey into mead, and malted barley into beer. The word "yeast" originally referred to the froth that meant fermentation was taking place. In the Middle Ages, this froth was also called "goddis-goode" because it came, presumably, from the grace of God. It wasn't until Pasteur took out his beakers and his swan-necked flasks and embarked on his classic wine experiments that the precise nature of all this fermentation began to come to light.

When yeasts in bread dough feed on the starches in the flour, the alcohol they create evaporates during the baking. But the carbon dioxide becomes trapped in the air pockets of the dough and causes the loaf to expand. Wild yeasts are fickle and weak and slow-acting; it used to take a couple of days to make a loaf of bread. For centuries, though, they were the only leaveners available. Quite often, bakers harnessed these wild yeasts simply by saving out a pinch of risen dough from one baking day to the next. Or else they went to their local alehouse and asked for some barm, the yeast-laden foam that floats on the top of fermenting beer. In order to give these sluggish wild yeasts a running start, bakers worked their pinch of flour or their dose of barm into a slurry of flour and water, then set it in a warm place for several hours. This sponge, named for its bubbly texture, allowed the yeasts to multiply and gain vigor before undergoing the prodigious task of raising a mound of dough.

Not until the late nineteenth century did brewers learn to culture reliable, potent strains of yeast in the laboratory. Soon after, companies started manufacturing packaged, dehydrated yeasts selected specifically for bread baking. Today's commercial baking yeast is a pure, concentrated strain of *Saccharomyces cerevisia,* which means "brewer's sugar yeast" as it was first isolated from a sample of barm. Virile and hearty, it can raise a batch of dough to double its size in under an hour, a time-saving measure that has all but done away with the preliminary sponge step. But seasoned bakers like Lena persist with the sponge, for its long, slow period of fermentation improves the texture and deepens the flavor of their finished loaves.

The mashed potato in Lena's sponge adds another layer of complexity to the bread's flavor. It also makes for a refined, delicate crumb, and its moisture helps keep the baked loaf from going stale. The irony is that its presence in the recipe is a remnant of hard times, for historically, potatoes tended to end up in the bread dough during grain shortages when flour was in short supply. Potatoes cheaply bulked up the loaves, making them stretch to feed another hungry mouth. As for the water left in the pot after boiling up the potato, it is rich in starch. When nineteenth-century bakers in Europe started working this liquid into their bread doughs, they found it made a particularly nourishing broth for the infant yeasts to feed upon, and they passed this trick on through the generations.

In the morning, Lena returned to find her sponge a seething mass. She stirred it down with a wooden spoon, then trickled in a tablespoon of oil, a large pinch of sugar, and a scant tablespoon of salt. Then she started working in four cups of flour, cup by cup. When stirring the dough became too troublesome a chore, she turned it out onto her flour-dusted breadboard and began to knead, adding sprinklings of additional flour from time to time to keep the dough from sticking. This act of kneading — repeatedly folding the dough toward you, pushing it down and away with the heel of one hand, then giving it a slight turn with the other, fold, push, and turn, fold, push, and turn — renders order out of chaos. In contact with liquid, the proteins in flour form into strands called gluten. At first, these

strands are just an intertwining tangle, a skein of
yarn left in a room with a no-longer-bored cat. But
as you knead, the tangled strands unfold, come into
alignment, and lengthen. They slowly become elas-
tic, able to stretch like coiled springs as the yeasts
give off gas, which allows the air pockets in the
dough to expand instead of burst.

Lena stood with her feet braced against the floor,
her shoulders hunched over the counter, absorbed in
her vigorous, waltz-tempoed kneading. Without
looking up she said in her low, quavering voice,
"Raising good bread is like raising good children."
Which is how I gathered that this Touch of hers is no
coddling, tentative nudge. Rather, it has a sensibility
about it, both patient and firm. "And honey, I do
mean raise," she added. "Only suns and moons and
congregations rise."

In ten minutes her dough grew silky and
smooth. She cradled it up in her knobby fingers,
then put it into a lightly oiled bowl. Lena knows
yeasts are fussy about temperature. They are most
active in places that are warm, but not hot, for anything much over 125 degrees will kill them, and they
slow down miserably when they get too cold. So she
set her bowl in a nice quiet spot by the stove, blanketed it with a kitchen towel, and left it to rise for an
hour and a half, maybe two hours. Halfway through
the rising, a gray-haired, hunched neighbor dropped
by for a visit, and Lena said, "Don't just stand there

in the doorway, you're letting a draft in on my bread dough. Come on in, I'll fix you a cup of tea."

When the dough had doubled in size, Lena deflated it with a sweep of her hand, turned it out onto the counter, and shaped it into two taut, round loaves. These loaves she let rest, again covered, in lightly greased eight-inch cake rounds (regular loaf pans will do) for three-quarters of an hour, until they nearly doubled in bulk. This second rise gives bread its characteristic fine texture, turning the honeycomb web of big air pockets created during the initial rise into a tightly woven mesh of tiny ones. Finally, she made two shallow slashes in the top of each loaf and set them to bake at 375 degrees.

Forty-five minutes later, a perfume of malt and toasted wheat drew Lena back into the kitchen. She opened the oven door and peered in at a pair of fully bloomed, amber-tinged rounds of bread. "Well, forevermore," she said with a soft gasp as she placed the loaves on a rack to cool. And the youthful, tickled expression on her geriatric face told me that the first time, the thousandth time, these products of her own two time-weathered hands never failed to take her breath away.

For one of the most enduring delights of making bread is that every loaf bakes up differently, and for reasons that even the microbiologists with their agar plates and their electron microscopes have yet to understand fully. What makes bread rise is no longer in the realm of the unknowable for us, but there still remain elements of surprise and mystery in a home-spun loaf of bread that only add to its charm. So, while I've little doubt that a basic understanding of bread-making mechanics can help a person acquire Lena's touch, I wouldn't want anyone to get *too* pre-occupied with all of these inner workings. Especially considering my last conversation with Lena. We started talking about bread, and I told her all about fermentation processes and cultured yeast strains and commingling gluten strands. To which she replied, "Heavenly days!" She was quiet for a mo-ment, and then she added, "I'm not so sure a body'd want to know all that if they were just starting out. The weight of it might just seize them up." Indeed, there's plenty to be said for pushing up your sleeves and starting in, for learning to bake by feel.

At Ease with Strangers

DINERS IN DIJON LINE UP at bistro doors each spring for *morilles à la crème*. Piedmontese housewives seek out a few fresh *porcini* to add to their bubbling pots of *risotto* in October. And in the Ukraine, men on trains discuss the prospects of the *pecherytsia* season like Yankee farmers talk about the weather. These wild mushrooms, and more, flourish throughout North America. Rich veins of them pop up in our forests, along our country back roads, often in our own backyards. Yet most shoppers in the United States know edible mushrooms only as the little white buttons in the plastic boxes they pull from their grocer's shelf. Few of us think of wild fungi as delicacies. We regard them with suspicion, fear, and disdain if we consider them at all.

As a culture, we owe this fungophobia to the British, from whom we also inherited an unfortunate national tendency to overcook asparagus and leg of lamb. While the rest of Europe dined merrily away for centuries on foraged mushrooms — developing passions for scads of varieties and learning to avoid the baddies — the British ate only button mushrooms. All the rest were toadstools. And toadstools, as everyone knows, are poisonous. Evil. Deadly.

Which is why wild mushrooms bring to mind visions of witches' cauldrons, wings of bat and eye of newt. From the compost and digestion of the forest floor come sordid scavengers who feast on the dead and parasitize the living. Our parents warned us of imminent danger should we so much as touch a slimy toadstool, let alone eat one.

Such notions shaped my own dubious opinion of wild mushrooms, and the botany lectures in my college biology classes did little to raise them in my esteem. I learned to divide fungi into a taxonomist's list of Latin terms: ascomycetes, basidiomycetes, discomycetes, gasteromycetes; names all committed to memory, but meaningless for any useful purpose other than passing a test.

I did discover that what most people call a mushroom is really just the reproductive structure, known as the "fruiting body," of the mushroom proper. The actual mushroom is a network of hair-like filaments, called a mycelium, which is often too fine to see with the naked eye. These filaments interweave and spread through the soil (or tree, or whatever else they choose to feed on), and eventually meet up with another mycelium of the same species. Provided all adequate conditions of nutrition, humidity, temperature, light, and parental consent have been met, the two unite and a mushroom forms. This mushroom rises up and disperses its spores, which go on to find a suitable landing spot and develop into mycelia themselves. But I considered this to be nothing more than a nice bit of trivia, like knowing that a praying mantis bites her paramour's head off before they mate.

Then I learned of the dreary evolutionary paths that brought mushrooms into their special niches as agents of decaying fortune. Stories like that of a small, reddish brown mushroom, aptly called the Corpse-finder, because it emerges from soil enriched, among other things, by decaying human remains. Legend has it that a detective used this odd mycological fact to help him solve a murder case. He spotted a patch of these morbid mushrooms, dug in the ground underneath them, and unearthed the corpse of the victim. A second fungus, the stinkhorn, has a most telling odor. In an extraordinary testament to the cunning of evolution, stinkhorns mature in hot, humid weather and impart their fetid aroma throughout the air. They reek precisely of a warm, ripe, steaming pile of manure. Flies alight on these slimy mushrooms like, well, like flies will do. A stinkhorn is at the mercy of the fly to multiply. While most fungi release their spores into the air, just as a milkweed sends its seeds adrift on the wind, stinkhorn spores are not airborne. They adhere to the body of the fly, who disperses them when he departs to seek his next meal on some cow-pie. Another hideous character is the Wasp Eater, an ill-mannered guest who arrives uninvited and overstays his welcome. He invades a buried, hibernating wasp, consumes it while it slumbers, then sprouts a mushroom from the mummified remains of his polite host.

As you can imagine, sordid particulars such as these did little to bolster my gloomy image of mushrooms in general. Some professor may have mentioned the prospect of eating wild mushrooms, but I wasn't about to take anyone up on the idea.

I'd made up my mind about mycologists, too. The very bottom-feeders of the biological sciences. If they had even an ounce of self-respect, they'd be out studying mountains lions or grizzlies or other fauna higher up on the food chain. To spend an entire career analyzing fungi was to admit an unseemly predilection for death and decay.

And I'd been around. I knew what kind of folk took to eating wild mushrooms. I'd read about a certain farmer on the southern coast of Washington State in the mid-seventies. He puzzled over the steady flow of vans with California license plates that pulled up alongside his property. The occupants kept asking to take a stroll across his upper pasture. He thought these visitors were stopping to admire the way the field out back of the barn nestled up against the gentle Cascade foothills. Or perhaps they were taken by his swanky herd of polled Herefords. Three prize-winners last year at the Puyallup Fair, you know. But what those long-haired tie-dyed beatniks were really after was a little brown mushroom called a Liberty Cap. The grassy hummocks of that cow pasture annually produced one of the largest crops of magic mushrooms in the Pacific Northwest. Imagine! A thousand tickets to a psychedelic experience, free for the picking. The NO TRESPASSING signs went up as soon as he learned the truth. Liberty Caps may be all-natural and fat free, but they are still illegal. Now the crop withers and dies each year unharvested, and the field is nothing but a shrine to unfulfilled psyche-delic trips.

Yes, I knew to cast aspersions on those who ate wild mushrooms. Even that naughty Alice. A nibble of one side of the toadstool made Alice grow larger, and a bite of the other made her grow small. Served her right. Perhaps a taste of yet another allowed Lewis Carroll to invent her in the first place. I'd rather not think of such dabblings with altered states.

I must admit that some professionals have used wild mushrooms with good intentions. Country doctors collected Alcohol Inky Caps and prescribed them to the village drunk. Tippler's Bane, they called them. These common mushrooms made a tasty dinner for the patient, but a nip at the bottle ruined a perfectly good meal. You see, Alcohol Inky Caps block the liver's ability to detoxify alcohol. The offender's symptoms were mild and transient, nothing more than light-headedness, vomiting, and a few heart palpitations, but they sufficed to sober him up for a day or two. Come to think of it, Alexander Fleming stumbled onto a dandy little mold when he found *Penicillium*. Which means a musty fungus ushered in the age of modern medicine. But such examples are the exception, not the rule, are they not?

My sentiments exactly. Until I tried my first morels at a restaurant on the Long Beach peninsula in Washington. But for that restaurant, the town might be just another anemic fishing village at the mouth of the Columbia River. The chef had made her reputation by paying tribute to the indigenous bounty of the region. Local mushrooms appeared on her menu alongside oysters, salmon, fiddleheads, and wild blackberries. I came in hopes she might share the culinary secrets that made people from Seattle drive three and a half hours to her table just for dinner.

My memorable dinner marked the culmination of an audition for a position in the kitchen. After I spent the evening working on the sauté line, I was told I could take my meal in the dining room. Off came the apron, the chef's jacket and hat, leaving me in jeans and a T-shirt. The kitchen had been hot, and I had been nervous. I wiped droplets of perspiration from my forehead with the back of one hand and gave a few stray strands from my braid a once-over with the other. I followed the hostess to a small corner table, quite the eyesore, I imagined, as I dined alone.

No one asked me what I wanted to eat, but a few minutes later a waitress delivered a rose-rimmed dish of sautéed sturgeon filet with morels and Cabernet. Until that sturgeon came to rest on my plate that evening it had called home the chilly waters of Willapa Bay behind the restaurant. The black, honeycomb-capped morels came from the mossy floor of a nearby spruce forest. I'd sliced those mushrooms earlier in the day and wondered just who would eat such curiosities. I poised my fork, ready to eat them to be polite.

The sturgeon was sublime. Perfectly cooked, impeccably seasoned. And the morels! Meaty, intense, like a smoky Christmas ham. I knew right then, I was hired for that six-days-a-week, twelve-hour-a-day, four-fifty-an-hour job. If not, surely the kitchen would have sent me out a hamburger.

I was right. I took to that first cooking job with fervor. And in addition to the chopping, slicing, boning, toasting, frying and sautéing I saw in that kitchen, I learned wild mushrooms make good eating.

When I arrived it was mid-May, the peak of the morel season. I discovered that this dainty fungus causes quite a sensation among mushroom fanatics. Her tenure is short and sweet — each spring she ushers in the season, as one veteran mushroom hunter put it, "when the leaves on the oak tree are the size of a mouse's ears." In New England, morels show up when the apple trees start to bloom. You'll find them in old orchards, under dead elms, and in recently burned areas, but they blend so imperceptibly into their surroundings, they are easily overlooked. In the Cascades, hunters seek Forest Service maps of last summer's fires with hopes of finding morels. And at the annual morel festival in Boyne City, Michigan, contestants sally forth at the sound of a gun to collect as many morels as they can find in ninety minutes. The record stands at over nine hundred.

At the restaurant, we were never so fortunate as to obtain them in such abundance. But we had a local forager named Ed who brought them in by the boxload on occasion. As the summer unfolded, the morel harvest waned, then stopped altogether, only to make way for the new season's bounty. Ed arrived at the back door of the kitchen, cradling a basket of his goods between plump, doughy arms. He was an odd sort, just the type I had imagined might spend his time culling through the bowels of the forest floor. In his mid-thirties, he could not have stood more than five feet tall. A faded, threadbare beret held a jaunty angle atop his head, failing to contain the shocks of wild red hair that shot from beneath it. Bilbo Baggins personified, I wagered. I opened the door and invited Ed inside as I'd done a half-dozen times that summer.

"Boss in?" Ed asked, directing his attention to the floor, anxiously tracing the outline of a tile with the toe of his workboot.

On hearing his voice, my employer put down her knife and looked up from the Chinook salmon she intended to filet. She left the patient sprawled out on the operating table, grabbed a towel, and walked across the kitchen, extending her still-damp hand. "Ed, good to see you. What've we got today?"

"Chanterelles're up."

She looked though his basket, smelled and poked and pinched a few of the orange trumpets for freshness. Satisfied, she went out the swinging door to the bar, opened the register, and returned to pay Ed cash on the spot.

He took the payment in a grimy, stubby paw and shoved it into his pants pocket. "'Preciate it," he mumbled, turning to leave.

"Wait a minute," I blurted. "Can I go with you sometime? To hunt mushrooms, I mean." The memory of those first morels propelled me. He was a strange one, indeed, but he knew his mushrooms. And what I wanted was a teacher like him. Not one of those bookish grad students who knew whether gills were adnate or decurrent, but someone who knew how to track down an edible wild mushroom and bring it in for supper. "I won't raid your spot or anything," I continued. "I'll even close my eyes so I won't know how to get there. I just want to learn where they grow. You know, the terrain they like, and how you identify them."

He looked me briefly in the eye before turning his gaze down to the tiles. "Well . . . um . . . well . . . I'll have to see," he responded, and disappeared.

After a few days of warm, hard rains, Ed showed back up on the back porch with a fresh crop of chanterelles. In the midst of shucking two hundred oysters, I looked up and said hello. He grew pale, nodded, and then went straight to his business transaction.

Outside on the porch a gray, shriveled woman, her head covered in a shawl, peered through the screen door. She had barely more pounds than years. "Can I help you?" I asked. She pulled back from the doorway without a word and vanished.

Ed finished his deal and walked out the door. I assumed he didn't want to confront me with my recent proposition. But a few minutes later he returned. He removed his beret and handed me a crumpled brown bag. "My ma says it would be okay if I took you mushrooming."

We set the date for the following Monday, ten o'clock, and Ed dashed back out the door. I looked inside the paper sack and found it full of fresh young chanterelles, still wet with morning dew. Through the window I saw his car drive away. The tiny silhouette in his passenger seat lowered the shawl from her head.

By Monday morning I had all but reconsidered. What kind of a guy asks his ma for permission? But the chanterelles enticed me. And I couldn't blame Ed's mother for checking me out. After all, these were sacred grounds I was asking to see. I decided to count myself lucky to have passed muster.

The old lady must not have thought all that highly of me, though. Ed told me we were headed for their *second* best spot, not their prime hunting grounds. He drove up a narrow, washed out logging road and parked the car. With our heads bowed to the earth, we strode through the woods on a deer trail, our prey far more elusive to me than any six-point buck.

Ed pointed off the path. I saw nothing. He crawled under a fallen tree, took out his pocket knife, and harvested four rotund, cinnamon-capped mushrooms. "King Bolete," he said. He turned one of the mushrooms upside down and showed me its cream-colored, spongy underside and bulbous beige stem.

"There's one more." I pointed, excited.

"Won't do," he said, and kicked the cap off my prize. A hundred maggots writhed within it. "Too old. Gotta git 'em when they first pop up, or they git buggy." He sliced one of his boletes in half length-wise to reveal its pure, untainted flesh. "Nice, eh?" He smiled, a few teeth missing. "My ma's favorite. You take one."

I declined, didn't dare go poaching his mother's mushrooms. I did not find any boletes of my own until I moved to New Hampshire three years later. Europeans know this mushroom by many names — King Bolete, porcini, cèpe, steinpilz, *Boletus edulis* — but whatever they call it, they speak of it in adora-tion. Its earthy, rich flavor complements any stewpot, and cries out for a hearty glass of red wine to accom-pany it. Corpulent and fleshy, these mushrooms pop up in pine forests in droves after summer and autumn rains. The cap of a King Bolete can exceed ten inches, its weight, more than a pound. Just a few can make a hearty supper for the whole family. I wondered how Ed's mother fixed them as we bushwhacked along.

The deer trail had long since dwindled to nothing. I pointed to every mushroom I saw, a child on her first Easter egg hunt. "What's this? And this? And that?"

Each time, Ed replied, "No good. No good. No good." Finally he stopped and motioned toward a lovely mushroom rising out of a pile of fallen leaves. "Here's one you should know." It stood alone. Slender, elegant, lily-white, as alluring as a prima donna at the ballet, its diaphanous veil wrapped modestly around its stem. It looked delicious.

"It's beautiful," I gasped.

Ed shook his head. He cleared his throat and recited:

> Lovely to look at
> Delightful to hold
> But if you eat it
> Your heart will stop cold.

I laughed, not at all expecting this awkward character who peddled his wares at the restaurant to recite poetry.

"My ma taught me that," he said. "Destroying Angel. Guaranteed to kill you." He pointed out its defining marks — the white gills, the fragile veil around the stem, and he uprooted the mushroom, revealing the egg-shaped sac from which the stem emerged. The sac was the conclusive evidence, for all *Amanitas* bear this telltale cup. Many are poisonous, some lethal. Experts, with microscope and acid test, can key out a few edible mushrooms from this family. But since a case of mistaken identity can be deadly, I don't find them worth the bother.

We crossed a clearing and came upon another logging road that meandered along a trickling creek bed. Orange mushrooms dotted the moss-covered shoulders of the road as far as I could see. So this was Ed's number-two chanterelle spot. I couldn't help but wonder what the mother lode looked like.

Ed plucked one of the vase-shaped mushrooms. It was fleshy, almost rigid, and smelled of apricots. In the Pacific Northwest foragers with grander schemes than Ed harvest them by the thousands. They sell them to commercial brokers, and they also pickle them in brine, ship them off to Europe, and receive top dollar for what the Germans call *Pfifferlinge*.

Into our baskets they went. Broad, mature mushrooms, some of them spanning the breadth of my hand. Ed was a practitioner of good mycological husbandry. He showed me how to cut the mushrooms at the base so as not to uproot them and damage the mycelia in the soil. And he made sure to leave behind plenty of tiny buds, no bigger than my fingernail, to mature and disperse their spores for next season's crop.

An hour later, we hiked out of the woods with five pounds of chanterelles. Ed dropped me back at the restaurant. "See ya around," he said, eyes focused straight ahead. "Too bad I couldn't take you to my other spot, but you know how it is."

"Hey, don't worry. Tell your mom thanks for me, would you. And thank you. I learned so much today, I really did."

Ed fidgeted with his cap, mumbled good-bye, and drove off. I walked home, my bag full of mushrooms, my head full of new-found mushroom lore. I had a perfect mental image of the chanterelles I'd seen in the ground. Surely I would recognize them anywhere. But later, when I went out into the woods alone, memory did not serve. Were those chanterelles growing out of that dead stump? This fat one might be a bolete, but Ed's mushrooms weren't red underneath, and they didn't turn blue when he cut them, did they? My confidence melted. I came back empty-handed.

I needed Ed around again. That Piedmontese housewife probably learned about mushrooms at her mama's knees, just as Ed had. She would no sooner mistake some odd orange fungus for a chanterelle than she would an apple for a tomato. But such mothers' knees are hard to find in these parts. I had to learn the hard way. Wild mushrooms were strangers to me, and it took more than just one foray into the woods to feel at ease with them. I pored through books, took notes, cross-referenced. But the real lessons came from hours of crawling around on forest floors, seeing mushrooms for the hundredth time instead of the first. I brought specimens to seasoned foragers for second opinions until I trusted my own judgment.

I've never been back to Ed's private chanterelle reserve; don't know if I could even find it. I have, however, learned enough about chanterelles and boletes and shaggy manes and black trumpets and chicken-of-the-woods to keep myself rich in mushrooms. And although I'm almost embarrassed to admit it, when it comes to my favorite haunts, I'm as territorial as Ed's mom. After all, good mushroom grounds are like good fishing holes. Once you stumble onto a hot spot, you don't go sharing it with just anybody.

Wine by Numbers

YOU CAN ALWAYS TURN to numbers when it comes to drinking wine. At a corner in a trendy restaurant, a man in a double-breasted Armani suit, a thin leather tie, and pointy Italian shoes runs a finger down the price column of the wine list, and stops at the highest number. Three digits? All the better. "I'll take a bottle of this Montrachet," he says, snapping the list shut with a flick of the wrist and flashing the gold of a fat Rolex. You'd like to inform him that he has botched the pronunciation: the name does not rhyme with "hatchet," but you sense he would not welcome the correction.

Across the room a fastidious old woman, be-spectacled and tight-lipped, her high-collared blouse fastened with a cameo pin, scans the same column of prices looking for a suitable wine on the opposite end of the scale. She gives you a frown of disapproval, then a sigh, and says, "I'll just take half a carafe of the house rosé."

Other diners know better than to let dollar signs dictate their wine selections. Consumer's guide ratings, not price tags, are the numbers that direct them. A savvy lot, these people have done their homework, memorizing text from guides such as *The Wine Spectator* and *The Wine Advocate*. These publications, part Bible, part Farmer's Almanac, part society rag, lead readers through the confusion of vineyards, vintages, and varietals to Truth in fine wine.

Enlightened readers have learned that steep prices aren't always a sign of quality, for expense can just as easily reflect an aggressive marketing campaign. They cringe to see fine wine go to waste on unappreciative palates, shake their heads at poor fools who fritter away money on overvalued wine to nurse equally inflated egos, and they count their blessings for a liberal wine education. Yes, these wise consumers know wine buying can be risky business. Why tread on unknown oenological turf when the experts, trained to judge wine on both technical merit and artistic impression, can spare your palate the disappointment of a bad tasting bottle? With a swish and a gurgle of wine over tongue, these masters rate the contestants on 100-point scales, culling the bad from the good, the naughty from the nice.

Their taste buds have perfect pitch. In a sip of Cabernet they do not merely detect mint, they can distinguish peppermint from wintergreen. With one taste of Burgundy, they'll note a hint of plums. Not just any plum, but damson in particular. The butterscotch overtones in a well-balanced Napa Valley Chardonnay could earn it a score of 94. But the burnt-sugar flavor that lingers in the Sonoma bottle warrants a twelve-point deduction.

Wine critics accompany these ratings with detailed tasting notes, allowing the buyer to know a wine's attributes before ever opening a bottle. Voluptuous, ripe, and full-bodied, they write. Intense, evocative nose. Dazzling legs that go on forever. You can't help but wonder if they've been sampling wines in bottles, or wenches in brothels. Yet consumers trust the verdicts of such finely honed palates without question, and don't you think they should, if the best their own taste buds can muster is bitter, sweet, sour, and salt?

I have to admit I found these wine guides indispensable when I worked at an upscale restaurant in California. We had what you might call a serious wine list. Wines rare and pricey, a candy store for connoisseurs. Any given night I might uncork the likes of La Tâche or La Tour from France, not to mention some of the finest boutique wines the Napa

Valley had to offer. Because I kept abreast of the current wine literature, I could ask diners how they enjoyed their Chablis *premier cru,* with its steely character, elegant personality, luscious fruit. Could they not smell the apple blossom in the nose? They replied, yes, now that I'd mentioned it, they did. And I bit my tongue as I decanted a young Cabernet. Infanticide! Though its fruit was lush, a wine with such brooding, muscular size and backward bouquet needed at least five more years in the cellar. Indeed, I knew so much about these wines, I forgot I'd tasted precious few of them. In fact, personal taste was a criterion I'd completely overlooked.

That is why the owner at the wine store in Yakima stumped me when she said she preferred the Russian River Ranches to the Les Pierres. We were talking about the Chardonnays of Sonoma Cutrer winery, of course. Everyone knew that the Les Pierres vineyard consistently reigned supreme in the wine guides, but she said she thought the Russian River Ranches tasted better. Tasted better? I dismissed her silly notion out of hand. Who cared what she thought? Les Pierres made the critics swoon.

I fondled the bottle, studying its label in the dim light. Surely she'd read about its copious quantities of honeyed fruit and toasty oak. All the critics preferred it to its wallflower sister from the Russian River Ranches. How could she think otherwise? And here I thought she'd know her wines.

I had stopped at the wine shop late on a gray November afternoon while home visiting my parents in Washington. I'd lingered over bottle after bottle, searching for a classy California Chardonnay for the next night's dinner, but just browsing, really. Wooden crates of wine, stacked one atop the other, lined walls of crumbling gray stone. Four claw-foot mahogany tables crowded the room, displaying an assortment of fine bottles, placed label-up on their sides like spokes on wagon wheels. I noticed I was her only customer during the last few minutes before closing.

She said it again. "Yes, the Russian River Ranches is a far more memorable bottle for me. What's the occasion?"

"I need a really special wine. I'm preparing *pasta e vongole* tomorrow night."

"Ah," she said. "Spaghetti with clams." She pursed her lips, accenting cheekbones chiseled despite their sixty-odd years. She wore a black wool sweater, as dark as her wispy hair. The dim light gave a soft luster to the strand of graduated pearls around her neck. "You're thinking of the Les Pierres? I think it might overpower the meal. I've got just the number, though. An Oregon Pinot Gris. Would you like to try a taste?"

I followed her across the room to the cash register. She lifted an opened bottle of wine from its terra-cotta cooler, showed me the label and poured

a couple of inches into a glass. I held it to the light
and inspected the wine's clear, straw-colored hue. I
stuck my nose into the glass, inhaled, and smelled
ripe fruit. Apples, I thought, as I sipped, although
I'd have been hard-pressed to tell whether they were
Gravensteins or Pippins.

"Very nice," I said. "Um, how much does it
sell for?"

"Eight twenty-five."

"How come so cheap?" I asked, disappointed.
I'd been prepared to shell out thirty dollars for a
Chardonnay.

"Not cheap, a good value," she corrected me.
"Those who think only an expensive wine can be a
good wine have a great deal to learn."

I said yes, I knew, and I told her about the man
in the Armani suit. She smiled. I sensed she'd met up
with a few of these characters herself. My eye caught
sight of a bottle of Bordeaux on the table. I wanted
to say that a sip of that Bordeaux was no better than
a tea bag in the mouth, didn't she think, and could
she believe how the winery's standards had plum-
meted in recent years. If she'd read the October
Wine Spectator, certainly she would agree.

Oh, I did love to sound erudite among the wine
cognoscenti. But at that moment, in the presence of
her eight-dollar Pinot Gris, so light and fruity, so
unassuming, I realized my words would fall flat with
a thud. So I took another sip and asked, "Since you

don't pay any attention to price, and you don't put much faith in the critics, just how do you know a fine wine?"

She looked at me, eyes wide, puzzled. "Why, I prefer to judge a wine by how it tastes."

She glanced at her watch. It was past five o'clock. "Would you like to try a red Rhone?" Without waiting for a reply, she walked to the front door, locked it and placed the "Closed" sign in the windowsill, then disappeared into the back room.

As I waited in silence, I looked at her vast treasure trove of bottles and thought what an unlikely operation she ran. Certainly a shrewd wine dealer would not approve of her strategy. A broker for whom Bordeaux futures were a commodity, no better, no worse, than pork bellies or lentils, would pack his bags in an instant and move to a metropolitan area. He'd hang a sign out a window in Seattle or San Francisco, or at least in some quaint tourist town like Mendocino, somewhere easily accessible by deep-pocketed city sophisticates.

He would know that if you wanted to make a profit, you did not open a boutique in a redneck appletown like Yakima, amid rows of fruit warehouses and a dusty, vacant train station. You did not try to do business on the block known to be the promenade of the town's dozen or so whores. Not with an inventory like hers, you didn't. Perhaps you sold chewing tobacco and cigarette papers, but not Burgundy and

Graves. Likewise, you did not talk your customers out of thirty-dollar Chardonnays and into eight-dollar good values. And you did not close up shop in order to share an old red with a young snip.

But if wines were your passion and not just another stock option, you did. Yes, I thought, you did these things and probably more.

She emerged with a dusty old bottle, a wedge of cheddar cheese, and a box of crackers, which she placed by the cash register. Then she upended an empty wine crate, set it down by her desk, and motioned to me to have a seat. The wine was a Vieux Télégraphe Châteauneuf-du-Pape, ten years old. I wondered whether I could resist the temptation to see what *The Wine Spectator* had to say about it. As she opened the bottle, I noticed her hands, terribly crippled and disfigured by arthritis, but still able to wield a corkscrew with a bit of coaxing. She seated herself in the Windsor chair behind her desk and poured us each a glass of the Rhone, dark and inky, with the shades of brick-red that wine acquires with age. We toasted to fine wine.

The wine tasted earthy, spicy, felt heavy in my mouth, smooth as it slid down my throat, warm as the south of France from which it sprang. The flavors lingered on my tongue long after I swallowed. I took another sip and the taste intensified. It was, truly, the first time I'd let my own palate taste a wine. Across from me, she smiled, eyes closed. I broke off a corner of cheese, set it on a cracker and wondered when she would speak.

"Don't misunderstand me," she said. "Price lists and hundred-point scales are all well and good, especially for wine brokers and investors and the like. But when it comes to actually drinking the wine, a five-point scale will do."

The lowest grade a wine can score, she explained, is a One. A One indicates a wine you would rather spit out than swallow, a wine you'd be hard-pressed to toss into a bowl of salad greens, let alone drink from a glass. In fact, the word "vinegar" comes from the French phrase *vin aigre*, or "sharp wine."

A One is not so common today as it was once. Almost every commercial wine is at least tolerable upon release. Vintners have access to such an array of technology: centrifuges and filtration systems, sterilized steel tanks and genetic clones — it is quite difficult to make a truly bad wine. Not to say it can't be done.

I described to her the way the wine in the chalice at Communion made your mouth pucker and your tongue go numb. I figured it must be a One. My mother once asked our priest if the church might take up a special collection to improve the quality of the house pour. Perhaps a fruity Chianti or a light Beaujolais might better serve the parish. After all, it was the Blood of Christ. He reminded my mother, politely, but firmly, that Communion was a Holy Sacrament and not a cocktail party.

She agreed with me, that wine sounded just like a One. She picked up the Rhone and tilted it in my direction. "Mmm, please," I said, sliding my glass across the counter.

"And then there is the wine I call a Two," she said. "A wine is a Two when a glass of it is better than no wine at all." Open a Two and find a readily drinkable wine, to be sure, but if you had your choice of ten wines, it would probably do no better than ninth pick. Just the sort of wine, I thought, I drank with my friends in college. Our options were few, our wallets were slim, yet we needed a cheap wine to wash down good swill. Yes, more than once I'd found myself quaffing a Two.

She turned in her seat and pointed to a crate of young Burgundy. "Don't go thinking an expensive wine could never be a Two." A rare bottle of red may strike the perfect balance of acid and oak, tannin and fruit, but the point is moot if, to you, it tastes like Robitussin. The palate knows what it likes, not the pocketbook.

She explained she often thinks of a cheap Two as cooking wine. Lavish restaurants love to go napping their seared filet mignons with *sauce bordelaise* made from some twenty-dollar bottle of Cabernet, but a fine claret is best sipped from a goblet, not sopped up from a plate. After the marinating and braising and saucing are all said and done, just about any old wine will do. But do cook with at least a Two, for when you feel like simmering up a *coq au vin* or *boeuf bourguignon*, you can douse the pot with a Two, then pour yourself a glass. It takes the drudgery out of standing over the stove to stir.

She paused to take another sip of the Rhone, raising her eyebrows over her glass. "And that is why," she said, "I prefer to do my cooking with a Three." A Three, she told me, is everyday wine. Young, fruity, and cheap. In France they have two names for it, perhaps because they drink so much of it: *vin du pays*, which means "country wine," and *vin ordinaire*, "ordinary wine." In Italy they call it *vino da tavola*, "table wine."

A Three is meant to accompany the meal, which is the real reason to drink wine in the first place. Wine heightens the flavor of foods, it piques the appetite. Any Frenchman worth his salt will tell you that without wine, even the best-laid table seems incomplete. But when a flask of wine appears at supper, even the most humble repast can satisfy.

No one minds if you spill a little Three on the table when you pour. No harm done, no precious dollars gone to waste with every drop. And the stains in the tablecloth? Such a good, hearty meal deserves a little memento.

As I listened to her words, I realized I already knew how to drink a Three. You can swig it with anything, anytime. Drink it from mismatched stemware with a pot of spaghetti and a loaf of crusty garlic bread. From thick glass tumblers with a take-out pizza on the floor of your living room. Straight from the bottle with cold chicken, blue cheese, and apples at a picnic in the woods.

She informed me it's even permissible to say a Three tastes like grapes, an accusation you would never make of a finer wine, she said with a wink. For when the fruit of the vine comes into the hands of a skilled vintner, wine-making goes from industry to art. A master seduces his grapes, enticing them to give forth essences of black cherry, blackberry, and cassis. Or strawberry, chocolate, olives, hazelnut, and tobacco, not to mention vanilla, apple, pineapple, melon, leather, and fig.

She stopped, out of breath. I told her she forgot plums and mint. She gave me a grave look. "You understand, then, what an insult it would be to a vintner to say his creation tasted simply of grapes."

I reached across the counter and topped off our glasses. She gave her wine a swirl in the glass, peering deep into the vortex. "These premium wines are what I call Fours. A Four is a wine that you wish you could drink more often than you do." Unfortunately, she explained, the bottle is either too expensive or too rare, or you happen to be one of those poor souls who does not drink enough wine. When you taste a Four, you want to drink it down fast, because you can't get enough of it. Instead, you force yourself to ease it down slow, because you want to savor every drop.

With a Four, it doesn't hurt to let the food show-case the wine. "If every night I could go home and sip a glass of old Bordeaux, I would need just a few slices of good bread, a wedge of cheese, a pear perhaps, and I would go to sleep a happy woman," she said.

She set her glass down on the counter and we sat in silence for several minutes, thinking about pleasant dreams and old Bordeaux. Finally she said, "Four points will suffice for almost all the wine you'll ever meet, but there will come a time when you will stumble on a Five."

The measure of a Five goes beyond flavor, beyond age, beyond price. It goes beyond the bottle, even. You might say a Five is a Four's leap to immortality. It takes more than mere flavor to make a wine a memory. The company, the setting, the food, all have to be just right. No oenologist, with his tools for measuring brix, and specific gravity, and oxidation, can ever calculate the dimensions these other components add to wine.

You probably won't recognize a Five when you first taste it. Only later, usually during the course of the bottle, but sometimes after days of reflection, will you come to understand that you have savored a Five.

She leaned closer to me. "Drinking a Five for the first time," she said softly, "is not unlike the first time you make love. The wine may in fact be a bit flawed, but it will seem perfect. You will never be able to drink another bottle without thinking back on the first time you had it."

A bone-dry Pinot Blanc might become a Five if old friends drink it on the beach with raw oysters shucked on the spot, eaten raw, sand and all. If a couple shares a bottle of Champagne in the midst of the Mojave to toast the desert bloom, most likely they'd say that bottle was a Five. "My first Five was a '45 Talbot," she said with a hint of a smile. "But I am a woman of discretion, and that's all I'll ever disclose of the memory."

She picked up a cracker and snapped it in two. Our glasses stood side by side, only a ruby droplet remaining in each. When had we finished the bottle? I checked the time, quarter past six, and told her I really should be going. I decided to buy a bottle of her Pinot Gris. She was right, I said, its light, tart flavor would pair beautifully with my clam sauce. I thanked her for sharing the Châteauneuf-du-Pape. So rich. So rare. So perfect. Such a pleasant way to spend a blustery afternoon. And by the way, what did she think of it?

"This old Rhone?" she asked, slowly tapping a gnarled finger on the side of the bottle. "From now on, I think it is a Five."

On Tossing a Caesar

THE PROPER EXECUTION of a Caesar has not always been a source of controversy. Brutus and his fellow Romans had no problem deciding how to off poor Julius. Hemlock? An asp? Out of the question. It had to be a dagger. But modern-day chefs cannot so readily reach an agreement when it comes to the execution of their own Caesar, a holy incarnation of romaine lettuce and garlic croutons. Should the egg be coddled or thrown in raw? Oh no, best dispense with it entirely. Anchovies, yes or no? Absolutely, but they must be mashed to a paste. Make that diced. Heretic! Don't let the smelly things within ten feet of the salad bowl. Dijon mustard? Essential. Never touch the stuff. And on it goes.

No one seems to care what the creator of the salad had to say on the matter. The eponymous Caesar was neither Julius nor Augustus. He wasn't even an emperor, but an Italian immigrant by the name of Caesar Cardini, who owned Caesar's Palace Restaurant in Tijuana, Mexico. The story goes, though some claim it apocryphal, that Cardini ran out of food on the Fourth of July, 1924, with a restaurant full of his Hollywood clientele, mink-wrapped, champagned, and hungry. He scrambled through the pantry and found romaine lettuce, Parmesan cheese, day-old bread, olive oil, and a few other kitchen staples. These odds and ends he turned into the special of the evening, much to the delight of his patrons in the dining room.

The salad's popularity spread north to Chasen's and Romanoff's, swank restaurants in Los Angeles, then up the West Coast and beyond. Today, whether it's a bustling neighborhood café at lunch or an intimate, gold-rimmed-china establishment for dinner after the opera, you can find Caesar salad on the menu. The International Society of Epicures in Paris voted it the greatest recipe to originate from the Americas in fifty years.

In the original version, Cardini arranged the inner leaves of romaine on a plate, filled them with croutons and drizzled them with dressing, intending the salad to be eaten with the fingers. Apparently, his patrons weren't partial to dirtying their dainty fingers, because Cardini soon started tearing up the lettuce and serving his house specialty as a tossed salad.

As for the rest of the ingredients, he insisted on only Italian olive oil and Parmesan cheese, hand-squeezed lemon juice, Worcestershire sauce, pressed garlic, freshly ground pepper, and a coddled egg. (A coddled egg, unlike a coddled child, has been dropped in boiling water for exactly one minute, so that it is more than heated and less than cooked.) Cardini put his foot down on the subject of anchovies. Leave them out! he cried. He insisted that a Caesar salad's strength lay in the subtlety of its flavors. Those with acute palates who detected a faint, briny essence had merely isolated the anchovy from the six drops of Worcestershire sauce that he put in the bowl.

But Cardini has been in the grave for decades, and chefs have long since stopped heeding his decrees. Anchovies have become a permanent fixture in the Caesar salad bowl. Perhaps it's culinary Darwinism. Some chefs take even bolder liberties, thinking of a Caesar salad as a little black dress to be accessoried according to the occasion. They add Roquefort cheese, crisp diced bacon, tomato wedges, cubed chicken, olives, even breaded oysters. Others cringe. Leave well enough alone, they say. Call it the special of the house. Call it a substantial meal. But do not call it Caesar salad.

Perhaps none of this Caesar anarchy would have come about if the salad had been the invention of a

French chef instead of an Italian immigrant. In 1947, the Third International Congress of Gastronomy in Paris declared that *pâté de foie gras* must henceforth be served at its proper place at the outset of a meal, rather than later with the salad as some freewheeling chefs had become wont to do. Surely the congress would have had something to say about the preparation of a Caesar salad. Ask any classically trained French chef to prepare you a *beurre blanc*, and he will walk into a kitchen and make you a sauce out of shallots, vinegar, white wine, and butter. Assemble twenty Italian housewives in a kitchen, ask them to fix you chicken *alla cacciatore*, and expect tempers to flare and frying pans to fly, for each woman has her own idea as to how your supper should be made.

The disparity merely reflects the historical difference between the two cultures. Italian history is one of fragmentation. Separated by barriers of language, geography, and political rule, the regions of Italy developed in isolation. Italians don't even consider themselves to possess a national cuisine; rather, they speak in terms of Tuscan cooking, Sicilian cooking, and the cooking of the Piedmont, to name but a few. In comparison, France has a history of relatively long-standing cultural and political unity. François Pierre La Varenne laid down the tenets of *haute cuisine* in 1651 when he published *Le Cuisinier François*, and his disciples in the culinary upper-echelons have formed societies and followed most of his recipes to the teaspoon ever since. The professional chefs of Paris who served the aristocracy had all been through the same formal training. Finding themselves out of a job after the Revolution, hundreds of these men opened restaurants throughout France and other parts of Europe and dished out *coquilles St. Jacques* and *pommes Anna* to the common man.

The same reverence for tradition holds, I think, for American recipes with French roots. Take eggs Benedict, a classic brunch entrée first served in the late nineteenth century at Delmonico's restaurant in New York City. (Delmonico was not a Frenchman; he was Swiss, but he introduced French *haute cuisine* to Americans, and his chef created eggs Benedict at the behest of a customer who was bored with the menu.) Order the dish today off of any menu in the country, and you will find, underneath a generous ladle of *sauce hollandaise*, two jiggling poached eggs atop sliced, smoked Canadian bacon on a bed of split, toasted, and buttered English muffin. No fried egg on brown toast. No béchamel. No surprises. The chef decides only whether to garnish the dish with a sprinkle of chopped parsley or to slide a fresh sprig into the cleft between the two eggs, a corsage on décolletée debutante.

Order a Caesar salad and no telling what you'll get, for there are as many ways to make one as there are pairs of hands to toss it. While most people agree the salad has romaine lettuce, garlic croutons, and Parmesan cheese, everything else tends to be a point of contention. Even if chefs can settle on the ingredients, they'll stand around and squabble about the proper way to toss the thing. Not even Cardini's offspring, who since 1956 have made a comfortable fortune manufacturing dehydrated dressing mix — just add vinegar and oil — still make a Caesar salad in the original fashion. Yet restaurants seem to me to teem with Cardini apprentices who learned to toss a Caesar at the old man's side. Except, they admit modestly, they think they've finally out-finessed the master.

The first time I had an authentic Caesar salad, I was out to dinner with my soon-to-be husband. He told me we must have Caesar-salad-for-two; he'd heard the establishment made quite a production of it. We gave the order to our tuxedo-clad waiter, a nervous rabbit of a man with thinning hair and an even thinner mustache, and he replied, "An exquisite choice. We make our Caesar in the spirit and grand tradition of the original." He leaned toward us and lowered his voice. "If I dare say, we make it better."

He soon returned, wheeling an elaborate silver cart across the candlelit room. Heads turned toward us to watch the show. His cart, as tidy and polished as a surgeon's table, was laid out with an assortment of silver spoons, forks, tongs, chilled plates, and a wooden salad bowl.

He took a garlic clove, sliced it in half, and rubbed its cut edge against the inside of the bowl with a few dramatic strokes. With dexterous, dainty fingers he put anchovies into the bowl and mashed them with his fork. In went the romaine lettuce, just the tender, pale green hearts, neatly cut into bite-sized strips. Extravagant, to be sure, but even deer, who survive on acorns and tree bark all winter long, turn up their noses at the tough, dark outer leaves in June when they raid the garden, and nibble only the succulent lettuce hearts.

Our waiter baptized these young leaves with juice freshly squeezed from a lemon, then he anointed them with drops of olive oil. He waved his hands over the bowl, a magician, a healer, sprinkling it with a pinch of salt, giving it a few shakes of Worcestershire, a shot of Tabasco, a dusting of Parmesan. He gently slipped the egg into a tiny sauce pot of simmering water and cooked it for sixty seconds by the count of his watch. When he rapped it squarely on the edge of his cart, steam ushered forth from the crack.

His thin mustache twitched and beads of sweat glistened on his temples. I noticed I was holding my breath. He held his hands high over the lettuce and let the egg drop out in all its coddled glory, then tipped the bowl toward us so we could see the sunny yolk, broken, spilling out of its sac. He took his silver spoons and began tossing the salad violently, furiously, not just using his hands, but his whole upper body for momentum — he could have been conducting Tchaikovsky's *1812 Overture*. He set down his spoons, threw in a generous handful of croutons, gave the salad a final toss, then heaped it onto the chilled plates. He served it forth, an enormous brass peppermill in hand, and said, "Would the lady care for pepper?"

I nodded, exhausted. Diners at the table next to us applauded. So taken was I by the intensity of the performance, by its freshness, its immediacy, I could not initially process what I first tasted. Yes, though, a second bite, and there it was again. The look in Bert's eyes convinced me he tasted it, too. I forced a hard gulp and felt a long, viscous mouthful of raw egg white slither down my throat. So this was a taste sensation in the grand tradition.

I shied away from Caesar salads until I started cooking in a café where I had to toss them on a nightly basis. My employer had worked up quite a theory on Caesar salad. She saw it as a sort of culinary litmus test for all the courses that follow. If a restaurant serves an impeccable Caesar, diners come to feel at ease. They can rest assured both palate and stomach will be in good hands for the evening. Myself, I tend to judge by the soup.

"That is why we take such pains to make sure our house Caesar is a classic," she told me. She placed a wedge of lemon alongside the salad she had just shown me how to prepare, then used the folded corner of a cotton towel to blot a spot of dressing from the rim of the plate. "Of course, we've taken a few liberties with the original," she said. "Improvements, though, all of them."

In that kitchen we had a pragmatic approach to making Caesar salads. We prepared them in the kitchen, behind closed doors and with adequate lighting. We puréed the dressing in a blender so as to do away with runny egg whites. When all was said and done, I learned, a raw egg is just as good as a coddled one. The owner taught me to tear the leaves, not cut them. Put the croutons in with the romaine, she instructed; croutons are nice when they absorb a little dressing. Same went for the Parmesan; it is a key ingredient, not merely a garnish. Go easy on the dressing, she advised; no one likes drowned lettuce, but a salad lightly dressed is a culinary masterpiece.

When I left that place, I knew how to turn out what I would call a decent Caesar. But not an impeccable Caesar, for the dressing was a bit thick — too much like mayonnaise, and it was too mustardy for my taste. It would have been heaven slathered on a hard roll with shaved roast beef and a thick slice of tomato, but I was still looking for something else to coat my romaine lettuce. Which, according to my employer's theory, might explain why her doors were closed within the year.

Some time later I took a job at a restaurant that featured New American Cuisine. That meant, according to the chef, that it proudly took the traditions of American cooking to exalted heights. And if there was one thing that chef could do, he said, it was work wonders with a Caesar salad.

My new boss was a wiry, harried man who blasted about the stoves clanking pots and slamming sauté pans. He wore a starched white chef's jacket, a toque, and a white cravat, which was really a table napkin. He rolled it up diagonally and tied it around his neck in a smart knot. He dared not cook without it. More than once he stormed through the kitchen, "Where is my tie? I can't find my tie! I will not plate one entrée until I've found it!" This all seemed to me rather superstitious for such a progressive chef, but what did I know?

I obviously didn't know how to toss a Caesar salad, he bellowed at me on my first shift. When the order came up, I reached for the romaine and began tearing it into pieces.

"No, no," he said, summoning his patience; I was, after all, a new pupil to his culinary movement. "Leave each leaf whole. In the New American Cuisine, we believe that the less a product is manipulated, the more its natural flavors shine through. We take pains to let the ingredients retain a form closest to their natural state."

I agreed with this philosophy with all my heart,

but it was the middle of January. The lettuces in question were not tender young shoots harvested from the garden out back, they were overfertilized, platter-sized leaves off three-pound heads from a cardboard box. You want unadulterated? I ached to say. Why don't I just plop a whole head of romaine on the plate and let the customer have at it? Instead, I said nothing, and added handfuls of croutons and Parmesan cheese to the bowl.

"What *are* you doing?" he yelled. "The croutons will be soggy! You'll ruin the salad. And the Parmesan is a garnish. It does not go *in* a Caesar salad, it goes on top!"

I dutifully picked out the croutons and poured in a ladleful of dressing.

"More, more," he cried. "Don't skimp. People order Caesar because they like the dressing."

Obediently, I added more dressing, grabbed a pair of tongs and began to toss the salad.

"Ah! Ah! Ah!" he said in a frenzy, though I think he enjoyed the prolonged torture of it all. "You must use your hands. Caress the lettuce. The tongs will bruise the leaves." He grabbed the bowl away from me lest I do any more damage, and gently stacked the leaves, Lincoln log fashion, on a chilled plate. He draped a fat anchovy on top of the salad, and said, "There! A Caesar salad in the New American tradition. Such an improvement over the original, don't you agree?"

I did not, but I plated his New American Caesar salads like a good girl every night I worked. When I ate at home, though, I discovered a respectable Caesar could be made by cutting day-old French bread into small cubes, enough to make about two cups, and putting them in a large bowl. Heat a few tablespoons of olive oil, a pinch of salt, and a minced clove of garlic. After the garlic sizzles, pour the oil over the bread cubes and toss to coat evenly. Spread the croutons out on a baking sheet and bake in a 350-degree oven until they are nicely browned. You can also toss them in a skillet on top of the stove, suit yourself. I have to admit I've developed an unorthodox predilection for croutons toasted medium-rare, just a bit soft on the inside. They soak up the dressing like little sponges. I could easily forgo the lettuce altogether and make a meal out of soft garlic croutons and Caesar dressing, but cook them as hard or as soft as you'd like.

As for the dressing, you'll need an egg, raw or coddled to your heart's content, the juice of a lemon, a few dashes of Worcestershire, two cloves of garlic, and four or five rinsed anchovies. I realize raw eggs have fallen out of favor in some locales. If it would ruin your dining experience to eat a raw egg, leave it out and substitute a half teaspoon of Dijon mustard. You can purée these ingredients in a blender; then, with the blender still whirring, drizzle in half a cup of good olive oil. Add salt to taste. If you prefer,

mince the garlic and the anchovies, then put everything in a large salad bowl and whisk like mad.

Wash a good-sized head of romaine lettuce, tear
it up, and put it in your bowl. By all means use
hearts of romaine if you're feeling indulgent. Add
the croutons, a couple of generous handfuls of
freshly grated Parmesan, and a few grinds of pepper.
Toss to coat with the dressing, and serve four to six
people.

You should be quite pleased with the results,
though I've no doubt this salad is not as good as the
original. Then again, how could anything beat a
Caesar salad and a glass of Champagne on a Tijuana
summer night at the height of Prohibition?

No Ordinary Soup

A POT OF SOUP, when made with care, not only captures the essence of its ingredients, it manages somehow to transcend them. Just think of a ham bone and a pound of lentils, say, or a couple handfuls of egg noodles and the carcass of a roast chicken — these might seem at first like meager, unpromising foundations for a meal, yet a little thought and determination can turn them into works of genuine artistry. The ingredients bound for the pot need not be precious, then, but you should treat them as though they were.

Of course, you cannot merely toss into the kettle every scrap you come across, every vegetable in the refrigerator you deem not-quite-sorry-enough-yet for the compost heap, and assume that your soup will survive the assault. Success, after all, depends upon a musical interplay of flavors and textures on the tongue, and a mishmash of ingredients results all too often in cacophony and chaos. So instead of trying for a full-symphony orchestra in the pot, it is better to think in terms of a small but accomplished ensemble.

These thoughts rushed through my mind as I set about making the soup one afternoon at the little French café where I worked for a time. I must admit I was a bit nervous. Anxious even. I had been hired in spite of the fact that I'd learned to cook at the stove instead of at an *école de cuisine*. My employer was all for formal French training. She herself was the proud possessor of a framed diploma from La Varenne in Paris, not to mention that she had eaten at Lutèce.

Although I'd managed to convince her I could indeed poach a roulade of sole and make *sauce velouté* and tell by the touch of my finger when a filet mignon had reached medium-rare, soup-making was not yet an assignment with which I'd been entrusted. But her head chef was taking his customary Tuesday off, and we'd experienced a run on soup the cold, dreary night before. We had served every last ladle of the two-day batch he had assumed would tide me over during his absence, which left me to start in on a fresh pot. Solo.

What I needed was no ordinary soup. It had to be elegant, but not fussy; understated, so as not to overwhelm the courses that followed, but by no means bland. I wanted something indulgent, but not so extravagant as to require any excuses down the road for my spendthrift ways, and I wanted something quick to prepare, for I had a sizable list of other tasks still to complete before the dining room doors opened at five o'clock sharp. It did not help matters any that the produce delivery was not due until the next day, and the pantry was practically bare. I did manage to find a bag of long, slender leeks, though, and then I knew just what to do.

I trimmed and rinsed the leeks, discarded their dark, fibrous tops, and cut the tender white and light green part of each stalk into thin slices. I stewed these slices with a spoonful of butter in a heavy stock pot for a few minutes, until they glistened and grew sweetly fragrant. Next, I added some russet potatoes, peeled and diced, along with a drizzle of salt — I was measuring in restaurant-sized proportions, but you can figure on one large leek and one medium potato per person for a family-sized pot. I covered the vegetables by an inch with light chicken stock, brought the liquid to a boil, then turned down the heat and let the soup amble at a gentle trot, not a full gallop, for three-quarters of an hour.

I might well have been content, for my own dinner, to stop right there. I could have swirled a nubbin of butter and a handful of freshly chopped parsley into the steaming pot just before serving, and then I would have enjoyed the rustic, hearty dish known in homes throughout France as *soupe à la bonne femme*. Translated, this basically means, "soup, as the good-wife would make it." The French attach this *bonne femme* term to many simple, inexpensive preparations — mutton stewed with bacon and tomatoes, apples baked with sugar and butter, an omelet filled with onions and herbs — that the average housewife whips together with ingredients she always has in store in her larder.

But my employer had a penchant for smooth soups. Rich, creamy soups. She thought them more possessed of finesse than the chunky, brothy variety, more in keeping with the silver candlesticks and starched white tablecloths in her dining room. She had the full support of the wait-staff on this matter, though for a more practical reason: thick, creamy soups stayed put in the bowl. They didn't go sloshing and splattering all over the linens as they were set down on the table.

So once the potatoes easily gave way when I crushed them against the side of the kettle with a wooden spoon, I puréed my soup by passing it through a food mill. A blender would have sufficed for the puréeing, but I've never been a fan of that other kitchen power-tool, the food processor, for this particular task. It obliterates the potatoes and turns their starches into wallpaper paste. I poured the purée back into the stock pot, then gently re-heated it with a lace of heavy cream — for a four-or five-potato batch, a cup of cream is about the right measure, and sometimes you need a little more stock or water to thin things out to a sippable consistency. Finally, I adjusted the seasoning with a sprinkle of salt and some freshly milled pepper, and I had just the soup to fit the bill.

Certainly, nothing could be more refined, more luxurious on the tongue, than this velvety combina-tion of potatoes and leeks. The enriching touch of cream and the powers of the food mill transformed my goodwife's soup. These fillips are niceties, pre-sumably, for which the *bonnes femmes* themselves had neither the time nor the money, and they are what transport her supper dish from the tables of dockworkers and plowmen into the finest dining rooms in the country.

The French named this satiny soup *potage Parmentier*, in honor of the gentleman who helped popularize the potato in their land. They also refer to it as *soupe à la Parisienne*, because it has been a cherished fixture for generations on the menus of so many chic Parisian eateries. Chilled and sprinkled with chives it becomes the equally swank *soupe vichyssoise*, which made its debut as the darling of the American restaurant scene during the 1920s. (In spite of its name, this iced summer soup did not hail from Vichy, but from the Ritz-Carlton in New York City. It was the invention of Louis Diat, a French-born chef who missed his mother's cooking and named his creation after the famous resort town in his homeland.)

The French word *soupe*, by the way, did not always mean soup. During medieval times, the *soupe* was the slice of stale bread that you put in the bottom of the bowl, and the *potage* was the contents of the cooking pot that you poured over it. The *soupe*, then, was what sopped up the *potage*, although the two terms are now used interchangeably. For most of France's history, her people came in from the fields and sat down to nothing more than a bowl of soup at their evening meal. Which explains in part why it now amuses me that a soup should embody the essence of Parisian sophistication. And a soup based on leeks and potatoes at that! This, especially, appeals now to my sense of humor, for these vegetables did not always enjoy such a high station on the social register.

Although we Americans tend to think of the leek as exotic and rare, its beginnings in Europe were downright common. As a cultivated vegetable, the leek, *Allium porrum,* is older than written history. Just precisely when it first sprang up, and where, are horticultural questions that remain open to speculation. By most accounts, the leek is native to the eastern Mediterranean. The fleeing Israelites knew of it, for when they found themselves in the desert with nothing but manna to eat, they lamented the melons, cucumbers, onions, garlic, and leeks they had left behind in Egypt.

As to how the seeds became scattered across Europe, the prevailing theory holds that the Romans discovered leeks growing in Egypt and brought them as far north as England during their forays. There is, however, a small contingency who maintain that since leeks fare better in cool climates than in warm, they may well have originated in the north, and then been introduced by the Celts to the Mediterranean during their many early fits of wanderlust. Regardless of their origin, leeks became a mainstay throughout the Old World in the diet of the lower classes — a hunk of bread and a few slices of pungent raw leek were often all there was for dinner.

While the peasants with their hearty natures could stomach quantities of leeks, the wealthy nibbled them sparingly as a condiment, lest they upset their more delicate constitutions. The vegetable did, however, have its place in the apothecary's cabinet. The Greek physician Dioscorides prescribed them for congested lungs, for stopping nosebleeds and easing menstrual flow, and for curing the bites of venomous beasts, though he cautioned that large doses of leeks caused troublesome dreams and dulled the vision. A few drops of leek-juice dribbled into the ear, he advised, would alleviate the pain of an earache — almost two thousand years later, this is a claim that modern science has borne out. The leek, as well as its siblings, the garlic and the onion, contain sulfur compounds that do in fact have antibiotic properties, and they can be beneficial in treating ear infections.

The Roman Pliny mentioned thirty-two remedies making use of leeks. Among them, a poultice of the leaves would help heal burns, pimples, and ulcers, and injecting the juice into the nostrils could cure a headache. He thought them effective as an antidote to eating poisonous mushrooms, though I wouldn't recommend testing this out in the field. What's more, he praised them for counteracting drunkenness, and for their aphrodisiac properties, but he warned they were a bit windy. Another celebrated use of the leek, he wrote, was to impart a strong timbre to the voice, and Emperor Nero, who was quite the song sparrow, set aside days each month for eating only leeks stewed in oil.

If anyone can be said to have a long history of esteeming the leek, it is the Welsh. Still, the vegetable did not capture their hearts with its distinctive flavor so much as with its role in their folk history. Thanks to the leek, the storytellers claim, King Cadwallader's men won a victory over the Saxons in the seventh century. This mythical battle took place near a field of leeks, and during the onslaught Saint David appeared. He instructed the Welsh soldiers to wear leeks in their caps to distinguish themselves from their foes during all the sword-fighting and bludgeoning. To this day the Welsh celebrate Saint David's Day every March 1 by pinning a leek to their hats.

In spite of the leek's detractors, by the Middle Ages the stewpot bubbling away on every French hearth contained one or two of them for seasoning. Leek soup was such a staple during the thirteenth century that Taillevent, chef to King Charles V, didn't even bother including a recipe for it in his masterwork cookbook, *Le Viandier*. The soup was so simple, so commonplace, he declared, that even women knew how to prepare it.

Five hundred more years had to pass before the potato made its way into the French soup pot. A native of the Andes of South America, the Incas had been cultivating the *batata,* which we came to call the potato, for thousands of years before Pizarro's men first laid eyes on it during the 1530s. Soon after, the potato traveled across the Atlantic to Seville in the holds of Spanish ships, then slowly made its way northward through Italy, Andalusia, and into France.

Upon the tuber's arrival in France at the turn of the seventeenth century, few people were any too eager to grant it a welcome. The potato, *Solanum tuberosum*, suffered the misfortune of belonging to an ill-reputed group of plants called the nightshade family. (Its American siblings, the garden tomato and the bell pepper, shared in this same sorry fate, and they, too, met with a cold reception upon crossing the Atlantic.) When Europeans encountered the potato, they were familiar only with its Old World relatives, which they knew to be a sordid lot indeed: the bittersweet night-shade of old fields, whose poisonous berries could kill foraging livestock; the foul-smelling henbane, which when ingested was as toxic to humans as it was to chickens, although doctors used it topically to treat chilblains and gout; and the deadly narcotic bel-ladonna and hallucinogenic mandrake, which were the very herbs that witches added to their evil brews. Small wonder then, that the potato had a hard time overcoming its guilt by association.

The substance behind all this treachery is a toxic alkaloid called solanine, which the potato does in fact contain just underneath its skin in negligible quantities. With exposure to light, however, the con-centration of this chemical increases to levels that can be troublesome. The tuber conveniently comes with its own warning device, because light also causes the potato to produce chlorophyll under its jacket. Any areas tainted by solanine show up as the green blemishes your mother always told you to trim away or else they'd make you sick.

The first European potatoes may well have had slightly higher levels of this toxin than our modern hybrids. These amounts were by no means lethal, but they were sufficient to render an occasional mild rash, and that was enough to tarnish the potato's reputation severely. It came to shoulder the blame for a host of maladies: some doctors feared it caused syphilis, while others claimed it brought on leprosy. It made men lascivious, the Church proclaimed, and philosophers warned that it drove the weak in spirit to drink. Those brave enough to taste the potato declared it insipid and indigestible, which certainly didn't help garner it any favor. People kept trying to eat the tuber raw, and few ever thought to peel it. To gnaw away at a potato's tough skin, yawned the critics as they clacked their sets of wooden teeth, was an exercise in tedium.

For a short while agronomists entertained hopes that the starchy, mealy qualities of the potato might render it good at least for making bread, but their attempts failed miserably. They tried to bake doughs that consisted of just potato-meal, water, and yeast, and they ended up time and again with nothing but a heavy, gluey mess. They did not know that potatoes lack gluten, the protein found in wheat flour that gives leavened breads their characteristic springy texture. It wasn't until the eighteenth century that bakers thought to economize by extending their wheat-flour doughs with just a few mashed potatoes. They found to their delight that the resulting bread had a pleasant flavor and a delicate crumb, which explains why some seasoned home bakers still continue with the practice today.

So for more than a century after its arrival in France, the poor potato was a vegetable maligned. It served only as fodder for cattle, horses, and swine, and for the most downtrodden of peasants, who might as well have been beasts of burden themselves, for the lives they led. And then Monsieur Parmentier of the eponymous *potage* entered the picture.

Antoine-Augustin Parmentier held a post as an army pharmacist during the Seven Years War. He spent time as a prisoner of war in Westphalia, where his rations included the reviled potato. The tuber had become a staple throughout the German states by then, thanks in part to a little gentle nudging from Frederick William I of Prussia. His subjects were initially no more keen on the potato than were their neighbors across the Rhine. But in 1720, after a series of grain failures plagued his empire, the Prussian king ordered all his farmers to sow potatoes in their fields. When the peasants balked for fear of leprosy, he added that any violator would have an ear cut off with a sharp blade. A little edict here, a little famine there, a draconian measure or two, and the German lower classes found themselves potato-eaters.

When Parmentier was fed meal after meal of cooked potatoes, he found to his unending joy that he did not become a leper. His thoughts did not turn to debauchery, and he did not even suffer from indigestion. Upon his release, Parmentier noticed that the farm folk of the region all seemed plump and rosy-cheeked from their diet of potatoes, and he became convinced the plant could benefit his fellow countrymen, who were facing grain shortages of their own.

Parmentier returned to Paris in 1763, took a position as the head pharmacist at the hospital *Les Invalides,* and embarked on a tireless campaign to promote the potato. He gave elaborate dinner parties featuring potatoes at every course. He wrote articles championing the vegetable's nutritional benefits, and he distributed pamphlets among the masses, no matter that the empty-stomached masses were illiterate. He persuaded the bishop to declare the potato no longer poisonous, but miraculous, and local priests tried feeding potato soup to their starving flocks. The clergymen called this gruel "economy rice soup" to make it sound more appetizing, but the parishioners remained skeptical, and most of them refused to touch it. Apparently, they preferred starvation to the threat of leprosy any day.

Parmentier's position at the hospital allowed him direct access to King Louis XVI, whose support he finally obtained. They concocted a scheme to have a plot in the royal grounds sown with potatoes. With great ceremony, armed soldiers stood watch over the plants during the day, but they left the field unguarded at night. This soon aroused the curiosity of the peasantry, who came to figure that these odd tubers must be something worth stealing after all, and they began making off with potato plants for their own gardens.

These midnight raids doubtless boosted the vegetable's popularity, but it was the fall of the Bastille that clinched the place of the potato in French gastronomy. Suddenly, it was no longer just the uneducated peasants who went to bed every night starving and miserable. The revolutionaries found that with a little butter, a few herbs, and some salt, the potato became not only palatable, but republican. The stately Tuileries gardens saw their blue-blooded roses yanked up by the roots, and patriotic potatoes were planted in their place. Cooks began to treat the tuber with care instead of loathing, and the soul-sating *soupe à la bonne femme* became the nightly supper for many. Often as not, the goodwives simmered their leeks and potatoes in water instead of broth, for they hadn't a chicken bone in the house with which to make a stock.

When times improved, the legendary canon of French potato dishes soon followed — *pommes Anna,* Dauphine potatoes, potato gallettes, and of course the voluptuous *potage Parmentier*, with its underlying hint of sweet, subtle leeks playing so harmoniously against the earthy flavor of the potatoes. These dishes proved undeniably that with enough devotion, even a bowlful of adversity can become a delectation.

Unfortunately for me, I hadn't yet discovered any of this when my employer entered the kitchen on the evening I made my first soup in her café. So I could not appreciate fully the historical thrust behind the comment she made to me. She took off her coat, and started in as usual, examining the goings-on about the stove. She peered into bubbling pots, and dipped a finger into various canisters of condiments and sauces. She lifted the lid from the soup tureen, and breathed in a deep whiff. "Hmm," she said with guarded approval, "And what have we here?"

"I made some potato-leek soup for tonight," I said, without looking up from the pile of fresh parsley and tarragon I was mincing to sprinkle on top of each serving. I knew that scent, alone, was not enough to win her over.

She ladled a few spoonfuls of my soup into an espresso cup, blew on it softly, then gave it a sip. "Oh, *magnifique*!" she said, closing her eyes. "Delicious!" She helped herself to a second tiny cupful, and then she added, "But don't you suppose we ought to call it *potage Parmentier*? I doubt it will sell all that well, if the customers think all they're eating is potatoes and leeks."

A Secret Well Kept

TWO CUPS FLOUR, three teaspoons baking powder, three tablespoons sugar, a quarter teaspoon salt, six tablespoons of butter, one cup currants, and a cup of heavy cream is not my friend Mary's recipe for scones. She told me I could not give hers out, but it hardly matters. Even with Mary's recipe, I cannot make scones like Mary makes. I can make fine scones. Delicious scones. Tender, flaky, not too sweet. But they are not Mary's scones. My husband tells me to relax, quit being so hard on myself. My scones, he says, are every bit as good as Mary's, better even. While I appreciate his kind intentions, he knows upon which side his scone is buttered, and I'm afraid I can't believe him.

There are those whose lives revolve around a quest for perfection — at the ballet, in the bedroom, in a bonsai tree. Mary, who was once an employer of mine, has found it in an ethereal, buttery quick bread. She would never claim she makes an authentic scone, the rustic griddle cake that peasant women baked over peat fires in Celtic and Scottish Highland kitchens. Scones and bannocks, which were simply plate-sized scones, were the daily bread of the working class for centuries. Since few families could afford the luxury of wheat flour, they made their scones with just stone-ground oats or barley and water, and they were thankful to have even that much to appease the knot of hunger in their hollow stomachs.

Scones and bannocks also took more elaborate forms, variations I'm sure Mary wishes she could replicate, for they were remarkable cakes indeed. The Druids browned them over bonfires on the First of May and offered them to the spirits as a sacrifice in order to protect their herds and flocks from harm. In the Highlands at Halloween, bakers made bannocks laden with salt, and when they ate them, the resultant thirst induced dreams that foretold the future. And in Orkney, the groom broke a rich, buttery bannock over the head of his betrothed to consecrate the marriage. That night, hopeful bridesmaids slept with a crumb under their pillows to reveal a vision of their future spouse.

With such extraordinary powers, it is no wonder a good scone recipe became a household treasure, passed down from mother to daughter through
the generations. But Mary says her recipe is not a
guarded family secret, handed down by a grandmother of Scottish descent. And she did not sneak
into a London tea room to copy the recipe surrepti-
tiously from the kitchen files. If she had, she would
admit it, I'm certain, for she once mentioned helping
herself to a recipe for Belgian Bows, yeasty little pastry knots that are studded with black currants, rich
with ricotta cheese, and no longer the sole property
of a frail Belgian granny with whom she once baked.

The scone recipe is her own, a product of careful trial and error, of testing recipe after recipe: this
one has the rich flavor of cream, but its crumb is too
soft. This one has just the right taste of butter, but it
is not light enough. This one is too sweet, this one is
just plain bland. Yes, Mary knew what she was after
in a scone. She did not want to gussy it up, to take
wild liberties with white chocolate chips or sun-
dried cranberries or almond paste. What she created
is a classic — a scone tender, golden, and high rising,
rich with butter, and chock-full of tiny currants that
burst with tart flavor in the mouth.

Such is Mary's commitment to these scones, she
can't bear to compromise their integrity. In this, she remains firm. No, she will not heat your scone in the mi-
crowave, it only makes it tough. No, she will not

spread it with peanut butter and honey, do you think it is a sandwich for your lunch-box? And no, she won't give you any marmalade, marmalade's for toast.

Mary's partner Susan appreciates such resolve, but she believes a more accommodating approach goes over better with the customers. So just a few short months after they opened their ten-table café in the Sierra Nevada, they settled on a scone policy: Mary bakes them and Susan sells them. Ask Susan nicely and she will even spoon you up some marmalade, but not without glancing over her shoulder and whispering, Just don't tell Mary.

For her part, Mary has turned out thousands of scones, in batches of eight, six days a week, since their first day of business. Which, she concedes, is a great number, though she wouldn't have had to make nearly so many if Susan didn't eat one every morning for breakfast with a double-lattè.

Some would dare to call a scone a biscuit. Fortunately, they are mistaken. Don't argue with Great-Aunt Bea from Georgia, but a biscuit is not really the float-off-your-plate, melt-in-the-mouth morsel that she stirs up with fried chicken. Nor is it the crisp sugar cookie or the savory cracker that the English take with tea. And, although a French pastry chef would insist a biscuit is the tender sponge cake he rolls up into *Bûche de Noël,* he is not technically correct. Just how all these baked goods came to be called biscuits is anyone's guess. For biscuit means "twice cooked." *Pain de biscuit* referred originally to a mass of flour and water, baked, sliced, then baked again into hard, dry lumps to create a durable staple that could withstand the rigors of a long voyage. Soldiers ate *biscuits de guerre* on the battlefield. Sailors ate ship's biscuits on the open sea. These biscuits did not lose their flavor after months in a knapsack only because they hadn't any flavor to begin with. Certainly, if a biscuit were really a biscuit, no one would mistake it for a scone.

Today, perhaps the only biscuit that has anything in common with a scone is a slice of Italian *biscotti,* although we're more apt to call it a cookie. *Biscotti* have indeed been baked, sliced, then dried out in the oven, a process which renders them hard enough to withstand a plunge into a cup of cappuccino. The connection stems, then, not from a common mode of preparation, but from the fact that both scone and *biscotti* have become the darlings of coffeehouses across the country.

I gave Mary my *biscotti* recipe to use at the café. It's my mother's recipe, actually, full of almonds and aniseed and a shot of brandy. My mother has had that recipe for ages, though I don't know where she ever came across it. Surprisingly, not from my Italian grandmother, who did not make *biscotti.* That is why, my mother explains, my grandfather always kept half a sugar doughnut in the top drawer of his desk at the shop. He left it there until it got good and stale, then used it for dunking when he took his coffee every morning at ten o'clock. I can't recall that she ever told me what he did with the other doughnut half.

I came to hope my *biscotti* would make a nice trump card when I went to ask Mary for her scone recipe. She had shared several other recipes with me in the past — her bran muffins, her triple-chocolate cookies, even her Carey Grant Memorial Cheesecake, a token of unrequited love which she displayed next to his picture in the deli case. But I balked at even mentioning her scones. After all, they were her signature. She did consent however, albeit reluctantly and under strict terms. She washed the flour from her hands, jotted down the recipe on a scrap of paper, and said, "This is for you only."

I knew she meant it. For recipes mean power and renown. A secret well kept ensures indispensability. At least that's what Fernand Point thought, when he delighted his patrons at La Pyramide with *gâteau Marjolaine*, a multi-layered masterpiece of chocolate genoise, nut meringue, and praline buttercream. Cousin Ida believes the same when she brings her famous chocolate mayonnaise cake to Tuesday night bridge. It used to be French chefs gave out recipes, but forbade anyone to watch them cook. They invariably left out some *truc*, an essential step or ingredient — nothing so serious as to ruin the recipe, just an element of finesse without which the outcome was ordinary instead of sublime. Adding a tablespoon of vinegar to the water when poaching eggs is a *truc*. The acid keeps the eggs from spreading thin as they float in the saucepan. "Cold milk to a cold roux, hot milk to a hot roux" is another *truc*. It helps prevent lumps in your béchamel sauce. And setting a pan of water in the oven when baking a loaf of bread is a *truc* that produces a crisp, golden crust.

I didn't really think Mary wholeheartedly sub-scribed to this notion of secrecy, but I came to wonder after I attempted her recipe a few times, if perhaps she hadn't kept some *truc* up her shirtsleeve. What else could explain the tough, heavy doorstops I pulled from my oven? Had she omitted an egg? Reduced the amount of cream? I couldn't tell, but I sure couldn't re-produce her scones. Finally, I broached the subject with her. Um, would she mind terribly . . . just perhaps . . . did she think I might be able to watch her bake sometime?

"There's really nothing to see," she said, some-what evasively, it seemed to me. "I bake scones at five o'clock in the morning. Surely you don't want to get up that early just to watch."

The next morning found me outside the café, waiting. The wind howled. I turned up my scarf, pulled down my hat, and thrust my hands deep into the pockets of my jacket against the bitter chill of a storm that had pulled in overnight. I could see my breath in the dark and the first few snowflakes had started to fall. Mary and Susan arrived at five minutes to five. Mary pulled off her gloves, fumbled with the keys in the cold, then escorted me inside. "We wondered if you would show up. This weather and all," she said. The café seemed eerie and cold, too sterile. It wasn't the quiet, though it was quiet, and it would soon give way to the morning din, the steamroller rumbling of an espresso maker and the belching of a tired dishwashing machine, the clamor of plates being stacked and silverware dropped, and the chatter of the customers over Etta James's smoke-and-honey voice on the stereo telling everyone she's got some red hot lovin' cookin' in her oven. It was not that. It was the absence of smell that struck me. In that dark hour before the ovens fired up, the air was empty, and I had known the kitchen only by day when it brimmed with the intoxicating scents of roasting chickens and garlic and cinnamon and sourdough bread.

Mary took care of that. Before we so much as removed our coats she went to the front counter and flicked on the espresso machine. She put coffee beans through the grinder, made us each a *caffellatte,* and the bitter, burnt-caramel aroma of brewed espresso woke up the room. After allowing herself a slow, frothy sip from her mug, she set to work.

Around her thin waist went a faded, threadbare apron, and out came her measuring cups and spoons, a knife, a spatula, and her food processor. She turned the oven on to 400 degrees and placed a piece of parchment paper across a thick metal baking sheet. I held my mug near my face in both hands and let the warmth of the glass pass into my cold fingers.

Mary worked with the graceful conservation of movement that comes from the daily repetition of a ritual. She measured out flour, leveling each cup with a smooth scrape of her spatula. I'd been wondering about her flour. Perhaps it held the secret. The quintessential pastries of the British Isles — the scones, crumpets, muffins, sticky buns, and tea cakes — all share a tender texture which they owe as much to the English countryside as they do to the quick mixing and light touch of the hands that shaped them. Hard, red wheat, coveted for its high protein content by bread bakers who want a chewy, mouth-filling texture in a crusty baguette, does not thrive in the damp, foggy English climate. But British soil can support strains of soft, white wheat — grains which create the flour of choice for pastry chefs. Without yeast, the proteins in flour make batters and doughs tough. Soft, white wheat, with its low percentage of protein, helps ensure a tender crumb. In like manner, the white wheat of the Southern states, as opposed to the red wheat of America's heartland, gave Southerners the edge in making what they came to call biscuits.

Today, companies treat cake and pastry flours with bleaches, making them even softer still. They

market these flours under billowy names like Swan's
Down and SoftaSilk, names that promise housewives a tenderness in angel food cakes they'd have
thought possible only from a Betty Crocker cake
mix. But the label on Mary's fifty-pound bag of flour
read "Unbleached" and "All-Purpose." It had a protein content, then, that fell somewhere in the middle.
No *truc* in that.

Next came baking powder, which Mary doled
out by tidy spoonfuls into her work bowl. Baking
powder is what makes scones rise. It contains a mixture of sodium bicarbonate, an alkali, and cream of
tartar, an acid; both are products of grapes. When
the two meet with liquid, they react to give off the
carbon dioxide gas that pushes up the dough.

For some time I'd doubted if baking powder
alone could possibly account for the skyscraping
height of Mary's scones. The café nestled into a flank
of the Sierra Nevada at eight thousand feet in elevation. The higher the altitude, the thinner the air and
the lower the air pressure. The lower the air pressure,
the less resistance doughs have when they go to rise,
and the higher and faster they will expand. Mary
finds this lack of pressure a force to reckon with
when she bakes a cake. Unless she compensates by
cutting back on her leavening agents, her cake batters rise up and over the sides of the pan before they
have a chance to cook through. It is this same low
pressure that makes tricky work out of opening a

bottle of champagne at high altitude. The pressure from the gas bubbles inside the bottle is high, while the ambient air pressure is low. Merely removing the bottle's foil covering can be enough to send a cork flying across the room. I wondered if the high elevation that spelled disaster for her chocolate truffle cake could hold the key to her ethereal scones.

"Do you suppose it's the altitude that makes them rise so high?" I asked.

Mary paused, contemplating the idea. "I've never really given it much thought." Then she pushed out her lower lip, blew a dark, wayward wisp of bangs out of her eyes and shook her head. "Now that you mention it, I've baked them down in Berkeley, and I've never noticed any difference." She turned to Susan across the room. "Have you?"

Susan looked up from her pile of peeled potatoes. She stared out the window, trying to recall, I suppose, every single scone she had eaten since she began working with Mary, but no, she didn't think so — didn't think it mattered much at all.

Mary looked at me and shrugged. She threw a pinch of salt in the bowl, said, "It heightens the flavor," and then poured in carefully measured spoonfuls of sugar. After giving the ingredients a quick whir in the food processor, she cut chilled butter into bits, added these bits to the bowl, then coated them in flour. After a few pulses of the food processor, the butter was the size of small peas. Just as in pie crusts, chunks of butter in the dough help give scones their light, flaky texture.

"You don't have to use a food processor," said Mary. "If anything, they'll come out better by hand. But at five o'clock in the morning, I just don't have the time."

She drizzled some cream into the flour in a slow stream, again pulsing her machine. She reached into the bowl, tested the dough, and nodded, satisfied. "Here," she said, stepping back from the counter. "You feel." I squeezed the dough between my fingers. It was cold, a bit dusty with flour, yet soft and easily moist enough to cling together. "You want to mix the dough just this much and no more or your scones will be tough."

Mary dumped the whole mess out onto the counter and sprinkled in the currants. Gently, quickly, her whole body rocking rhythmically, she gathered the dough in her hands and kneaded it a half-dozen times, until it formed a ball. She patted the dough into a circle on the counter, three-quarters of an inch high, then basted it with a beaten egg. She divided the circle into eight wedges with four firm strokes of a sharp chef's knife, first making a cross, and then an X. "See how I cut straight down through the dough?" she asked. "You can saw back and forth, if you'd like. It's easier. Or slice from one side to the other. Of course," she said, slowly breaking into a smile, "you'll close up the edges of the dough, and your scones won't rise, but it's entirely up to you." She transferred each scone to her baking sheet with a spatula, and popped the tray into the oven. "That's really all there is to it."

I finished my *caffellatte* while Mary moved from scones to coffeecake to lemon tart. The ovens had warmed the kitchen, steaming up the windows. Inside, tiny rivulets of water trickled down the panes onto the sill, while wind-driven shards of snow pelted the glass from the outside.

About fifteen minutes later, a sweet, toasty odor emanated from the oven. Mary grabbed a worn pair of baking mitts and pulled out the scones, golden-brown and plump, butter sizzling on the baking sheet. She put a scone on the corner of the cutting board at Susan's work station, then offered the tray to me. "Surely you'll be wanting one of these."

I took one in my fingers, too hot to hold, and set it on a plate. I suppose an Englishman wouldn't even bother eating a scone without a spoonful of clotted cream. But I let mine cool a moment, then broke off a corner and ate a bite, warm and plain. "I have something to confess," I said. "I sort of suspected you of leaving something out. You know, giving me a bum recipe. But this scone is perfect. Not one thing could make it taste any better." Mary lowered her eyes and blushed. Then she too confessed. On her day off, when she was of a certain mood, she took her scone with a nice dab of raspberry preserves. Jam and bread, you see, never had it so good. Just don't tell Susan.

I moved to New Hampshire shortly after my baking lesson, and became determined to recreate Mary's scones in my own kitchen. I had a clear picture of Mary at her baker's table, working with a chemist's accuracy, and I tried to duplicate her moves precisely. I scraped my teaspoons level, weighed my flour, even calibrated my oven.

Still, the scones I baked were not the flaky, currant-studded carbon copies I had hoped for. I tried again, increasing the amount of baking powder to compensate for the atmospheric conditions in my low-altitude New England kitchen. That batch was not perfect either. So I gave it a third try, this time mixing the dough by hand. Like the Druids when they prepared bannocks, I even made sure to stir clockwise, in harmony with the rising and setting sun for good luck, but it didn't help. I tried again, and again. I made all sorts of subtle changes until Mary's recipe was turned inside out, and I ran out of currants and butter and patience. By then I had developed my own recipe for scones, and accepted the fact that I wouldn't ever learn to master Mary's. One thing I did learn, though. A carbon copy, no matter how fine the resolution, is never as good as the original. And I talked to Mary the other day. She said she doesn't bake my *biscotti* at the café anymore. No matter what she tries, it seems, she can't make hers come out quite so good as mine.

Enough Room for
Strawberry Shortcake

"IT'S A CRYIN' SHAME to be too full for shortcake."
Mr. Kavissi-ay looked up from his menu and said
this, as much to me as to Mrs. Kavissi-ay. That was
why he and the wife would each be having only a
cup of soup and a salad for supper that evening,
thank you. And they thought they would have just
enough room for a few slices of that lovely wheat
bread with sweet butter.

The Kavissi-ays were regulars at a restaurant in
Vermont where I worked. They dined with us at ten
minutes past five all summer long. Actually, they
made their reservations for five o'clock, and they
arrived promptly, but it took a good ten minutes for

them to cross from the front door to the back dining room where they liked to eat. He's pushing ninety, you see, and his wife isn't far behind him. They shuffled along, he with the help of a wooden cane, she with the help of his extended elbow, and by the time they reached their table they had worked up quite an appetite. So it was most unusual that they should pass up an entrée and go straight to shortcake, especially since they didn't indulge much in sweets anymore. Mr. Kavissi-ay had explained this to me apologetically on more than one occasion, knowing as he did that I baked the pastries at the restaurant. So don't take it personally, my dear, he often said, we just get plumb too full before we get to dessert.

His name was not really Kavissi-ay. Hers wasn't either, for that matter. But everyone at the restaurant called them the Kavissi-ays, because at the end of the meal he dabbed the corner of his mouth with the corner of his napkin, looked out of the corner of his eye at his wife and said, "And now it's time for a little sniftah of Kavissi-ay."

So that evening, after their carrot-ginger bisque and their mixed greens lightly dressed, and after two dishes heaped high with shortcake, I brought him a healthy pour of Courvoisier and her a coffee with cream. He held his very special old pale in one hand, and the craggy, wrinkled hand of his very special old wife in the other. He gazed into her eyes, she gazed into his, and they sipped their sips. They looked through the window at the gardens where we grew a good many of the vegetables that appeared on our diners' plates, and they saw rows of lettuces and sugar snaps and Swiss chard and a long patch of lush, green strawberry plants. Perhaps they even saw strawberries, plump, dead ripe, red to the center and still warm from the afternoon sun. But they probably didn't. Not from where they were sitting, anyway. Nobody could. But when I swung by their table to warm up her coffee, I could plainly see how happy they were to have had enough room for strawberry shortcake.

He leaned toward her and said, "Honey, let's never break up." The odds were in his favor, I would think, since just a week earlier, they had come in to celebrate their sixty-fifth wedding anniversary. In spite of the fact that they tended to get plumb too full before they got to dessert, I had baked them a special cake for the occasion. It was a triple-layered chocolate torte for two, filled with chocolate rum mousse and raspberry preserves. I garnished it with chocolate ruffles and a shower of fresh violets, and then we took it to their table and said we all hoped to be so lucky. A year later, I made sure to bake them short-cake-for-two to celebrate their sixty-sixth. I realized they only had so many opportunities for strawberry shortcake left, and it was a pity to waste one on some frilly chocolate cake.

People just seem to have a special place in their hearts for strawberry shortcake. Like chicken soup and mashed potatoes, it is one of those heirloom dishes that foodies have come to call comfort food. It is customers like the Kavissi-ays who make me believe these dishes call upon a nostalgic but genuine yearning for simpler times and slower paces. For in this tumultuous age of marital discord and corporate downsizing, crime and credit card bills, if there is one thing you can depend on, it is the food that good ol' Mom used to make. One bite of shortcake may not be as evocative as Proust's madeleine, but it will at least conjure up a Fourth of July picnic and bare feet, and that is no small accomplishment.

Yet dine out in early summer at some chic little spot, and chances are you'll see only strawberry meringues, or strawberries with crème brûlée, or *tarte aux fraises* on the menu. Or else the pastry chef will offer up a refashioned and refined version of shortcake, a symphony of hazelnut genoise, crème fraîche, and a mélange of red berries. Please pass the passion fruit sauce, he'll say, while trying to pass his concoction off as shortcake.

Why? Perhaps he's trying to compensate for having a lousy cook for a mom. But more likely because strawberry shortcake is an American dish. It is a long-standing sentiment among professional chefs that American recipes, while quaint and cozy, really do need to be sent off to finishing school abroad before they can appear in public. I suppose they aren't elegant enough for your average gourmand. Yet what is a French meringue but a mess of egg whites? Or crème brûlée but a bowl of pudding?

I took great pride in the fact that the Kavissi-ays' bowls of shortcake were the genuine article. By that, I mean a split biscuit, spooned high with lightly sugared strawberries and topped with softly whipped cream — the dish is too delicious to pull from the menu simply because it didn't hail from the royal courts of Europe. Some historians trace the dessert back to the Native Americans of New England. They cite the reports of Roger Williams, founder of Rhode Island, who wrote in 1643 that the Indians crushed strawberries with a mortar, then mixed them with meal and made strawberry bread. But the version that became an American classic did not evolve until more than two centuries later.

The dessert had to await, among other things, the development of the cultivated strawberry. For centuries, Europeans knew only the tiny alpine strawberry, *Fragaria vesca,* that grew wild in their woods. Gardeners brought the plant under cultivation during the fifteenth century, but they were unsuccessful in coaxing larger hybrid berries from it. Then reports began filing in from the Americas, describing wild strawberries growing in mouth-dropping abundance wherever there was room enough to lay down a foot, and specimens soon found their way back to Europe.

The Virginia strawberry, *F. virginiana,* made the crossing by 1600. A native of the eastern seaboard, its fruits possessed a lovely fragrance and flavor, but they were only slightly larger than the Old World berry. Then in 1712, a Breton naval officer by the name of Frézier, which by charming coincidence is pronounced like the French word *fraisier* — strawberry plant — brought back samples from South America that bore enormous but bland yellow berries. Thirty years later, a French botanist crosses this Chilean strawberry, *F. chiloensis,* with the Virginia strawberry, and the result is the ancestor of the cultivated berries we know today.

Still, strawberries remained a rare luxury in the markets. Families grew them in their home gardens for their own use, but the tender fruits were too perishable to withstand the lengthy travel time and all the jostling they suffered on their way to the grocer's stall. Then the locomotive steamrolled onto the scene, able to give fresh produce a gentle ride from hinterland gardens to city centers. In June 1847, the Erie Railroad milk train brought 80,000 baskets of strawberries to New York City in a single trip, and customers snapped them up with frenzied glee. By 1850, people were talking of the "strawberry fever" that was sweeping through East Coast cities. During this time, strawberry shortcake started making a fashionable appearance at the table, but it wasn't until after the Civil War, when a profusion of cookbooks streamed onto the market, that the dish became a summertime favorite in households across the patched-up country.

I managed to hunt up several splattered, dog-eared cookbooks from this era, and I felt tremendously pleased and validated to find that, by and large, the postbellum recipes for strawberry shortcake differed little from my own. They tended to agree, for instance, that three pints of strawberries, rinsed, hulled, and sliced, then tossed in a bowl with a handful of sugar, will serve six people. They often thought it best, as I do, to leave the berries out at room temperature for an hour to let the juices seep forth. And some, like the recipe in my grandmother's 1886 copy of *Mrs. Rorer's Philadelphia Cookbook,* even suggest mashing the berries slightly to help the process along.

These authors had no need to mention that the berries should be fully ripe and in season, for that was the only way strawberries came in those days. Today, the agricultural industry has succeeded in making strawberries available all year long, but these are under-ripe, insipid things, bred for transport, not flavor, and they bear little resemblance to the strawberries that made shortcake famous; although the dish may be indebted to interstate commerce and the railroads, it's now really only worth making when you have local berries.

Although I'm unsure as to the precise origins of the buttermilk biscuit recipe I use when I make shortcake, it is certainly in keeping with the recipes in many of these old cookbooks. Mine has you mix together in a large bowl two and a quarter cups of flour, two teaspoons each of sugar and cream of tartar, a teaspoon of baking soda, and a big pinch of salt. Next, cut a half cup of cold butter into small pieces and work it into the flour with your fingertips or a pastry cutter until it resembles rolled oats or coarse crumbs. My set of instructions actually reads "soap-flakes," which dates it back at least to the generation of women who knew what soap-flakes look like. Pour in three-quarters of a cup plus two tablespoons of buttermilk, and stir just until the dough holds together. Pat the dough into a rectangle three-fourths of an inch high, cut it into six rounds with a biscuit cutter or a drinking glass, or, even easier, into squares with a knife. Easier still, and perhaps more impressive, pat the dough into a nine-inch cake pan to make one giant shortcake, then bake it at 400 degrees until golden. Ten to fifteen minutes ought to do it for the small biscuits; count on an extra five or so for a big one.

When it comes to assembling the dessert, I find myself in near accord with the knowledgeable likes of Mrs. D. A. Lincoln and Miss Fannie Farmer of the Boston Cooking School in the late nineteenth century. I split the biscuits horizontally, still hot from the oven, and spread the cut sides with a bit of softened butter. Then I place the bottom halves on dessert plates or bowls and start spooning on the strawberries, letting some of the berries topple off onto the dishes, and allowing plenty of the syrup to soak up into each biscuit.

At this point, the two ladies would have you put the lids back on the shortcakes, then serve them up with plenty of cold, heavy cream poured all around. I, however, prefer my cream to be softly whipped, which is an embellishment that seems to have come into fashion only in the early decades of this century. None of my older sources make mention of the practice. You might think this is because the cooks didn't have electric mixers back then, but those ladies had big whisks and strong wrists, and they did the job in a trice for plenty of other desserts.

This little change in protocol occurred just about the time milk products started undergoing pasteurization in the United States, and I can't help but wonder if there is a connection. Unpasteurized cream has a rich sweetness to it that needs no further refinement. After pasteurization, a process that involves heating dairy products to sterilize them and lengthen their shelf life, cream loses some of its clean flavor. This is not an unreasonable sacrifice, since it also parts with its potential to give you typhoid or tuberculosis, but perhaps dessert makers started whipping the cream to make up in rich texture what they lost in taste. I don't know. I do know that it is worth seeking out cream that has not been ultra-pasteurized. Traditionally, pasteurization is performed at relatively low temperatures for a long period of time, say 172 degrees Fahrenheit for fifteen seconds, which imparts only modest changes to the flavor while still destroying disease-causing bacteria. Ultra-pasteurized cream is subjected to a high blast of heat — 280 degrees for about two seconds. The result is cream that keeps for weeks, but it has a discernibly cooked flavor, and it will never whip to the heavenly consistency of cream treated in a more gentle manner.

At any rate, the Boston contingency and I part company when it comes to the heavy cream. I put a pint of it in a chilled bowl while the biscuits are baking, then beat it with a balloon whisk or a hand-mixer until it begins to thicken. I add a dash of vanilla and a spoonful of sugar and continue whipping until the cream holds soft peaks. And when I build the shortcakes, I plop a generous dollop of the stuff onto the strawberries, crown each serving with the top half of its biscuit, set jauntily askew, then bring them to the table.

Now that is what I call shortcake, and with every forkful I can taste why it has brought such pleasure to so many generations. But even though the berries are fresh, the biscuits are hot, and the cream is cold, this may not be your idea of shortcake. It's not, because your mother, or your grandma, or whoever it was made you shortcake as a child didn't do it this way, and they were never wrong about these things. One of my married-in aunts has family in Arkansas, and she tells me everyone from Arkansas knows shortcake is made by tucking ripe strawberries between two delicate, flaky rounds of baked pie-pastry dough. This version is not without precedent, for in 1857 Eliza Leslie gave a recipe for just such a preparation in her popular *Miss Leslie's New Cookery Book*. New Yorkers who grew up eating at the legendary Lindy's might insist a proper shortcake is a towering layer-cake filled with the biggest berries you've ever seen. Perhaps for you, strawberries must dribble off a slice of buttery pound cake. Or else you wouldn't even bother to call it shortcake unless a few fresh peaches or blueberries or a generous scoop of vanilla ice cream were involved.

Then you'd best consider passing on my recipe altogether. Or at least consume it without expecting one iota of comfort from it, for it will not satisfy your spirit's hunger for that state of bliss you last felt while clinging to your mother's skirts. For the hunger is in the memory, not in the biscuit, berries and cream. And while the Kavissi-ays showed me how pleasing it can be to evoke a memory, I met up with another customer at the restaurant who convinced me it doesn't pay to go competing with one.

He and his wife, he told me, were on vacation from Georgia, and they certainly did appreciate the chance to enjoy a meal without that godawful heat they'd left back in Atlanta. They finished their entrées, and I came by to clear away their dishes. He untucked the napkin from his collar, pushed his chair back from the table to make a bit more room for the belly he'd filled with sirloin steak, and said, "Seems to me I remember something about shortcake on the menu tonight."

"That's right, sir," I said. "Strawberry shortcake."

"Yeah, well, of course you know real shortcake's made with peaches." He pursed his lips and smoothed a few strands of hair over his bald spot, giving considerable thought to the prospect of a dish of shortcake with just strawberries. He looked at his wife, then back at me. "You don't happen to have any peaches back there in the kitchen, do ya? You put some peaches in my shortcake, hon, you can park your slippers under my sofa anytime."

"Walter," his wife hissed through clenched teeth. "Leave the poor girl alone." She gave me an apologetic roll of the eyes, and I could swear she let loose with a sharp kick under the table for her husband.

I suppose I decided to take Walter on as a challenge, because I launched into a description of the merits of our strawberry patch. We were trying a new hybrid this year, I told him, and the plants were really thriving in the river-silt soil. Now, that could possibly account for the especially bountiful crop we were reaping, but the weather certainly hadn't hurt. Whatever it was, I said, the berries had been sitting out there soaking up the sun all morning, getting juicier by the minute, why he'd hardly even miss the peaches.

It kept him interested. He clasped his hands together and cracked his knuckles, limbering up for some more interrogation. "God forbid you don't send it out with a scoop of ice cream."

"Oh, no sir," I shook my head. "Whipped cream. We make it with fresh Vermont whipped cream."

He closed his eyes. "Ah, just like my mama used to make. And it's a good thing, else I'd send my Rose right back to the kitchen to whip me up some. Wouldn't I, Rose?"

Rose shifted uncomfortably in her chair, attempted a thin smile, and I wasn't so certain she would.

"Tell me," he said, "you make that shortcake with a biscuit?"

"Absolutely," I nodded smartly. I'd been waiting for this question and I figured I really had him. After all, doesn't every Southerner believe that at the heart of mama's home cookin' lies a batch of biscuits?

Maybe so, but they don't always belong with a bowl of strawberries, because Walter proceeded to bury his face in his stubby hands. "Well if that ain't just like a bunch of goddam Yankees," he said slowly. "You ask my mama, soon as she gets done rolling over in her grave, biscuits belong on the table with the ham and the gravy. Shortcake's made with thick slices of her heavenly sponge cake!"

I'd wager now that among the line of cooks in Walter's life, someone had a copy of Sarah Rutledge's *The Carolina Housewife* on her kitchen shelf. Published in 1847, it was a treasured text in many Southern homes, and tattered copies were passed down from mother to daughter to daughter. Indeed, its shortcake recipe gives you a tender sponge, made light and delicate with sugar and eggs.

Walter looked up at me in defeat and I was glad at least he didn't start to cry. "Well, what else ya got?" he said.

"We have maple-walnut pie, sir," I said feebly. "You might like that, it's a lot like pecan pie."

His wife gave him a comforting pat on the wrist. "She's right, dear. Why don't you try a nice slice of pie?"

He folded his napkin neatly on the table in front of him. "No, no. I guess I'm not hungry. I'll just take a cup of coffee and the check." Then he lifted a finger and gave it a stern shake. "But you should tell whoever needs to know, it's a cryin' shame to go putting walnuts in a pecan pie."

Forgotten Apples

A SCRAWNIER, MORE miserable excuse for a crop of apples you would never hope to find. Scabby, misshapen, ornery little things, all of them. Windfalls in the literal sense, the sight of them littering the orchard floor might seem less a stroke of good fortune than a testament to the measly wages of negligent husbandry. My octogenarian neighbor Dot, whose crop these apples happened to be, folded her arthritic hands across her stout bosom and said, "Dandies, aren't they?"

As for the trees from which these apples fell — ten of them, looming twenty feet high — their trunks are craggy and hollow with age, their branches gnarled and twisted. More dead than alive, it is a wonder they bore any fruit at all. Dot said she had a good decade on them and weren't they looking spry. She admitted she hadn't paid them much attention over the years, unless you count last August when she took a shot at a porcupine on their behalf. She found him perched up in the elbow of a tree branch, munching away on a summer apple and looking down on her with his big, dark eyes. Her eyes, however, are not what they used to be, and she regretted to say she missed the bugger.

Dot and I were gathering windfalls for her winter supply of cider. Sweet, of course, not hard. She'd never been a drinker. Or rather, I was gathering ratty apples into a droopy picker's bag that sagged low on my hips and knocked my knees, and Dot was following behind me with the help of the hoe in her hand for a cane. "Look there," she said, pointing a crooked finger at the ground. "You missed one." Dot hates to complain. Does not like to comment on the inequities of passing time. But she did mention, twice, it was making her sick to pieces to see her apples lie uncollected this fall, and all because of a hip that needed replacing before the rest of her.

For my part, I had come to Dot's New Hampshire orchard haunted by memories of the full-flavored apples of my youth in the Yakima Valley of Washington. I grew up knowing the valley as the Fruit Bowl of the Nation (probably because "Apple Capital of the World" had already been claimed by our neighbors to the north in Wenatchee) and took pride by association in the millions of world-class apples the region produced per year. But many of my childhood favorites were culls my mother bought cheap from the warehouses out on Fruitvale Boulevard. Yellow Transparents, Winesaps, Winter Bananas, Pippins, Gravensteins; apple fanciers now consider them heirlooms and they've all but disappeared from the marketplace.

At the turn of the century you could find hundreds of varieties of apples in the United States. Most of these were regional specialties, cultivated in pockets of the country by professional growers and amateur hobbyists and pie-making housewives. Apples best for baking, apples just for cider, apples to start the season off in July, and apples that made good keepers through the dead of winter. Some of these apples disappeared because they simply didn't taste like much, but others vanished because of some commercially fatal flaw — they ripened unevenly on the tree or came in irregular shapes or showed their bruises, and our pies and lunch-boxes and culture are only the duller for their absence.

After I moved to New England I started hunting around old cellar holes and traipsing across overgrown pastures in search of wild and forgotten apples. I managed to stumble onto a few gems, but most of my finds were mouth-puckering disappointments. Then I learned that apples don't breed true from seed. A thousand seeds will express genes from the same parents in a thousand different ways, but only a handful will lead to palatable apples. In order to propagate a variety, growers have relied for centuries on grafting: they bind a cutting from one tree onto a notch in the stem of another. Gardeners do likewise for roses, which are in the same family as apples. In fact, you can graft a rose cutting onto an apple tree.

Dot assured me I wouldn't find better-tasters than her McIntosh apples. I didn't admit to her that the McIntosh had never ranked too high on my list, didn't say how it bewildered me to find New Englanders so taken by it — September arrives and signs appear on country back roads, advertising Macs for sale, come pick your own. People bundle up in turtlenecks and plaid flannel shirts and head to the orchards. They enjoy free hayrides among the trees and sip complimentary hot cider while they fill their wooden bushels with Macs.

No doubt, the McIntosh is something of a horticultural warhorse, a staple for growers up here in the northern extremes of apple country, for it can withstand a New England winter and still blossom and bear fruit in the spring. But I couldn't help wondering if the festivities weren't just a diversion from the McIntosh itself, an apple I consistently found dull in texture and underwhelming in flavor.

Two hours and five bushels of windfalls passed before Dot let me have a taste of one of hers. She leaned on her hoe, reached to the ground and picked up another apple I'd overlooked, then wobbled for a few seconds to catch her balance. "Ah, here's a beaut." She gave the apple a quick polish on her shirt sleeve and began to pare it, wielding her pocketknife with a rigid, chapped hand. I tried to forget I had once seen her use this knife on a vole who had taken up residence underneath a head of Savoy cabbage in her garden. Beneath the scabs and knobs and bruises of the apple's mottled skin, creamy flesh appeared, stained with delicate capillaries of red.

As Dot whittled away she said the county extension agent had come to call a while back. He suggested she pull out her trees and plant a new McIntosh hybrid, a redder Mac that was not so prone to scab, an apple that could turn her a profit in a few years. She told him he shouldn't waste time talking long-term investments with old women, and he hasn't bothered her since. She handed me a slice. "Go ahead, try a taste."

I put the fruit to my lips, and all ten thousand of my skeptical taste buds were pleasantly surprised. The apple had a mouthwatering tartness, just sweet enough to keep my eyes from squinting. I'd read, but did not believe until that instant, that the quintessential Mac has a vinous flavor and strawberry aromatics. These traits helped make John McIntosh a wealthy man after he discovered the original McIntosh tree on his Ontario homestead in 1811, and they made Dot's neglected windfall one of the finest

apples I'd tasted in years. Dot merely laughed, and
the blade of grass she clenched between her teeth
flapped like a cigarette.

It occurred to me that perhaps Dot's hillside pasture brings out the best in a Mac; it may well have the
optimal McIntosh soil, the ideal weather, drainage,
sunlight, and host of imponderables that French vintners refer to as *terroir* when they explain that the vines
of the Romanée-Conti create the most exquisite wine
in the world, while just a few kilometers away the
grapes can only produce quaffing wine at best. But Dot
leaned toward me and shook a stern finger under my
nose. "Those new Macs," she scowled, "they've had
the flavor bred right out of 'em. Same thing happened
to those godawful Delicious apples that the greedy
farmers out in Washington make such a fuss over."

Since Dot let me take home half a peck of apples,
I decided not to mention that I know a few of those
greedy farmers out in Washington; they seem to me
like decent folks just trying to make a living. But she
did have a point. Although the Red Delicious is far
too common to be fashionable among the pomologi-
cal cognoscenti, I've always enjoyed the taste of a
ripe one. I'm not referring to the immense crimson
orb you find waxed to a shine at every supermarket,
but to the old Standard Delicious, an apple now
grown so scarce it, too, could be called an heirloom.

The original Delicious was a smallish apple with
pale red stripes, actually quite homely compared to

its progeny. During the 1870s a farmer by the name of Jesse Hiatt noticed a volunteer seedling sprouting in the middle of an orchard row on his Peru, Iowa farm. Twice he mowed it down, and twice it returned, so he threw up his hands and let it grow. Ten years later it bore a single fruit, an apple Hiatt called a Hawkeye. In 1893, Hiatt's Hawkeye won a prize in a national horticultural show. One of the sponsors tasted it, exclaimed, "My that's delicious, and that's the name for it," and proceeded to spend three-quarters of a million promoting his find.

As for the Golden Delicious, while it's not my favorite, I've seen my mother turn it into countless first-rate pies. The story goes that during the 1890s, the Golden Delicious, originally called the Mullins' Yellow Seedling, sprouted out of a cow pie in Clay County, Virginia. This is not terribly surprising, when you consider that the evolutionary reason for an apple's sweet flavor was not to tempt Adam in the Garden (scholars now suspect the forbidden fruit was actually an apricot, or perhaps a quince), but to encourage foraging animals to eat and disperse the seeds, complete with a dose of fertilizer. The Stark Brothers Nursery, which owned the Red Delicious, bought Mr. Mullins's tree for five thousand dollars in 1914. In order to keep their competitors from stealing cuttings before they introduced the apple to the market, the Stark brothers built a cage around their tree and paid a gardener a hundred dollars a year to tend it.

By the 1920s, grafts of both Delicious trees had made their way to the Yakima Valley, where farmers discovered the rich volcanic soil, desert sun, and brisk autumn nights grew them to perfection. But then marketers began crying to nurseries for a redder Red and a golder Golden Delicious. They begged to have their Delicious apples bigger and hardier and earlier, and they wanted smaller trees for easier picking. The results of years of genetic poking and prodding, coupled with the fact that apples tend to sit too long on the grocer's unrefrigerated shelf, are Dot's godawful Delicious apples.

Fortunately, a counter-trend has come afoot, the product of horticulturists and customers who've grown disenchanted with the sorry selection of apples in the produce aisle. One of my not-so-greedy apple farming friends out in Washington now cultivates Mutsus and Criterions and Galas and Braeburns. He says these new varieties make it rewarding, even plain fun, to be an apple farmer again; finally the public will buy something other than a red apple.

In addition, heirloom apples are making a comeback, fetching top dollar at farmers' markets across the country from customers intrigued by their whimsical names and charming histories — Sops of Wine. Maiden's Blush. Cox's Orange Pippin. Duchess of Oldenburg. I have yet to make a Brown Betty with a Bottle Greening, an apple named for the bottle of hard cider that field hands hid in the hollow trunk of the original tree. Nor have I packed a Bloody Ploughman in my lunch, the namesake of a thieving farmer shot by a groundskeeper for stealing apples from his master's estate. But I finally found a source for old-time apples in New Hampshire.

U-PICK 19 VARIETIES OF ANTIQUE APPLES, read a classified ad in my daily paper last fall. NO HAYRIDES. NO CIDER. NO MACS. I arrived, the only customer, at a hillside farm lined with rows of meticulously pruned, healthy young trees. But for the view of the Connecticut River and the blaze of autumn-forested hills in the distance, the orchard could have been another square in the tidy patchwork quilt of apple plots that blanket the Yakima Valley. On closer inspection, the trees hung heavy with apples in an array of shapes and colors and sizes like nothing I'd ever seen. A white-haired woman in an oversized barn jacket emerged from the house and greeted me with a deep, husky hello. "Nice day for picking apples," she said.

"I saw your ad in the paper," I said.

"Oh, the ad." She sighed and shook her head. "I'm afraid this season's it for us. Too many headaches." She gave a dismissive backhanded sweep of her arm toward the orchard. "This was all my husband's idea." She looked back at the house, where a thin tendril of smoke wound its way out of the chimney. Suddenly I felt the wind and wished I'd brought a heavier coat. "Course, you'll notice who's out here doing all the work," she said. "The painting, the thinning, the spraying, the picking. It's enough to break a body's back, and I bet I don't make three hundred dollars a year on it. My husband thought we'd get a bunch of yuppies up here. Get them reaching deep into their wallets for rare fruit like this."

From where we stood I saw that the trees had shiny silver tags around their trunks. Although I couldn't read the labels from so great a distance, they had names like Hubbardston Nonesuch, Westfield Seek-No-Further, and Pumpkin Sweet. "They come, all right," she continued. "Want me to take them on a tour. So up into the orchard we go, and I tell them all about my apples." I felt her hand on my elbow, leading me forward, up into the orchard so she could tell me all about her apples. "And after they take up all my time, what do they want to buy? McIntosh. Nobody wants to try anything new." She grimaced, and I all but expected her to spit. Then she looked me in the eye. "Tell me you're not looking to buy Macs."

"Not today," I said, then mentioned I grew up in Yakima, and drew a breath, planning to wax nostalgic on all the glorious apples of my childhood.

"Yakima? Good Lord, they have terrible apples out there." She furrowed her brow, and spoke as though to a naughty child she suspected of stoning songbirds, "I bet you even like that Red Delicious, don't you?" Before I had time to answer, to defend my valley's heritage, she apparently decided there was still hope for me. "Well, I suppose you might try an American Mother, it's sweet," and she changed course, steering me to the right.

As we walked, she showed me her Esopus Spitzenburg, Thomas Jefferson's favorite apple at Monticello. She pointed out her Fameuse, a tree with scarlet fruit that old-timers called Snow Apples for their stark white flesh. Nurserymen think the first Fameuse grew from seeds brought by French missionaries to Canada, she explained, and settlers along the shores of Lake Champlain cultivated it as early as 1730. She gave an affectionate pat to the trunk of a tree full of blotchy brown Ribston Pippins. Her personal favorite, she said. Not much to look at, but the English have prized it as a dessert apple for almost three hundred years.

When we reached her American Mother she plucked one of its gold-and-carmine marbled fruits from a lower branch. "Home orchardists during the twenties favored the Mother for her spicy vanilla scent and flavor of pear drops," she said, as if reciting an advertisement in a garden catalog. "The poor, dear Mother," she sighed and put the apple in my basket. "Nearly disappeared because she tends to fruit only every other year. But she's always been a good cropper for me."

I motioned to a tree covered with bite-sized yellow and red fruit. "Are those crab apples?"

"Crab apples? Hardly. Those are my Lady Apples. Louis the Thirteenth grew Lady Apples in his garden. And seventeenth-century ladies liked to carry them in their pockets." She rubbed her hands together briskly. "Be sure you pick a few Lady Apples."

Behind her I spotted a tree, its branches full of long, conical apples, so dark they appeared almost black. "And what's that one?"

"That?" she said, "That is the most good-for-nothing apple I've ever come across. Dry. Bland. Yuk." She paused, and cleared her hoarse throat. "It's called a Black Gilliflower. In Connecticut, where it came from, they called it a Sheepnose on account of its shape. My husband says he likes it with a slice of cheddar, but I think he's just being contrary." She glanced at her watch, then said she had to check her pies in the oven — she liked to use Rhode Island Greenings and Northern Spies, which I would find at the other end of the orchard.

She left me to my picking, and I started with Spartans and Paula Reds, then Blue Pearmains and Golden Russets, and kept on until I had twelve varieties. Out of curiosity I even picked a few Sheepnose, burying them deep in a basket so she wouldn't notice. I wondered what would become of her trees, now that she'd declared the orchard a failed business venture. Certainly my harvest made a motley collection, full of anemic colors and rough skins and odd shapes. I had three bushels, and not the slightest idea what I would ever do with so many apples once I got them home. Cynics would perhaps dismiss them as mere products of nostalgia, valuable only after time and distance distilled their essences into memories. Indeed they might, until they stood in an orchard on a brisk autumn day and tasted a Lady Apple, sweet and effervescent and gone in three bites. Or made a pie with Northern Spies. Or bit into a Ribston Pippin and discovered that the complex flavor of an apple can linger on the palate like fine wine.

I carried my baskets, one at a time, down to her back porch, where she stood waiting, examining my harvest from the doorway. I pulled out my wallet and thanked her for the apples, thanked her for all her time. "Those bushels aren't full," she said, folding my bills into her pocket. "I think you should go poke some more Lady Apples into the nooks and crannies." She began to shut the door, then reopened it and leaned out. "I'll still be here next year with all my trees," she said. "It's just, I'm done wasting my time on folks who don't appreciate 'em." She asked me my name and told me to give a call when September rolled around again. "You want, I'll let you come on back."

I promised her I would. And as I walked back up the slope to top off my basket, I made a mental note to ask my neighbor Dot to join me.

Fueling the Passions

MENTION THE WORD aphrodisiac, and most people start to giggle. If they think you are serious, they may start to giggle nervously, knowing as they do that Mrs. Emily Post does not consider the topic appropriate for polite conversation. This has not always been the case. Indeed, it is but a lingering vestige of Victorian decorum, for the subject used to be a respectable one, discussed on into the wee hours of the night by all sorts of learned and well-bred individuals.

Philosophers and poets of antiquity, Arab sheiks, Oriental herbalists and English physicians — these sages debated the merits of sundry comestibles and recorded volumes of nostrums for posterity.

Throughout the ages, hungry diners sat down to a sumptuous meal, then arose at its conclusion convinced they owed their renewed energies and elevated moods to certain particularly invigorating items on the menu. Many of these claims endured, emphatic and pervasive, for centuries. Some still do. And in spite of the best efforts of nineteenth-century gentlefolk to stem such base thoughts, you can't help but wonder why, if only for entertainment's sake.

Doubtless, the connection between food and desire is not a tenuous one. A bite of a ripe plum, sweet and dripping, the scent and sizzle of a steak on the grill, the luxurious feel on the tongue of melting ice cream — there is no denying that some foods have a power to arouse the senses. And appetite, which is triggered by as subtle a stimulant as the aroma of toasting bread, is controlled by the hypothalamus in the brain. The hypothalamus tells you when you hunger, when you thirst, when you are sated. In like fashion, it regulates your sexual drive. But these facts hardly suffice to substantiate all the notions of yesterday's scholars and voluptuaries. Though as I came to find out, they had reasons of their own for ascribing erotic powers to certain foods.

What started me in on this whole subject was the purchase at the farmers' market of a fresh black truffle — the savory variety, not the chocolate kind; I'll come to those presently. Truffles are actually stemless wild mushrooms of the genus *Tuber*. In size and shape they usually fall between a jawbreaker and a Ping-Pong ball, and they live out their elusive and fragrant lives underground. They choose, for reasons that continue to confound those who would like to cultivate them, to grow in symbiosis with the roots of certain trees — this chestnut tree, but not the one of equal size and age that stands twenty feet away; that twisted oak, but not the one up yonder on the hillside.

As precursors to love, truffles have enjoyed a long and noble history. The Greek physician Galen, believing them most conducive to sensual excitation, prescribed them accordingly to his patients. The Roman emperor Claudius is said to have relied on truffles to keep pace with his energetic wife Messalina, but the only certain connection between the ruler and mushrooms is that his next spouse Agrippina poisoned him with a dish of them.

Of the thirty-odd varieties of truffle, the best are the black *(T. melanosporum)* and the white *(T. magnatum)* ones of France and Italy, and at upwards of five hundred dollars a pound, they are currently the world's most expensive vegetables. The Romans don't seem to have known this pair, for they don't describe them within their texts, but by the eighteenth century both species had captured the attention of the upper class.

The French gastronome Brillat-Savarin wrote that truffles did seem to awaken erotic dreams equally in the sex that wore skirts and the one that sprouted beards. After Madame de Pompadour, the mistress of France's fifteenth Louis, suffered a series of miscarriages, she found herself weak and no longer eager to hear the royal knock upon her door at night. So she put herself on a diet that included truffles and celery soup in a desperate attempt to restore her passion.

The lore would have you know that Napoleon used truffles as an aphrodisiac. If so, it was probably in hopes of increasing his virility, rather than out of any desire to prolong the pleasure, for historians say he was quite perfunctory in this latter regard. With or without truffles, though, it took getting rid of poor Josephine and moving on to a new, young wife before the emperor could produce an heir. And some eighty years later in Florence, Pellegrino Artusi wrote in *La Scienza in cucina e l'Arte di mangiar bene* that he thought it best not to delve into the erotic side of truffles in his cookbook. But oh, the stories he could tell. Reading his cookbook today, I only wish he had divulged his tales.

Just what, besides word of mouth, did such a dingy little mushroom ever have going for it in the aphrodisiac department, anyway? Plenty. For starters, consider its shape. Until well into the eighteenth century, Europeans placed great store in what they called the Doctrine of Signatures. This theory, which traces back to the ancients but did not become formalized until the Renaissance, maintained that the appearance of plants gave clues as to their medicinal properties.

The yellow-flowered dandelion, for instance, evoked the symptoms of jaundice, so doctors used the plant for treating diseases of the liver. The convolutions of the walnut reminded physicians of the brain, so they valued the nut for sharpening the mind. It followed that a truffle, with its knobby, round form, would impart strength and stamina to key parts of the male anatomy. Same went for the equally testicular potato, until its New World exoticism wore off, while the shaft-like nature of a carrot, a leek, a spear of asparagus, and a stalk of celery endowed these vegetables with similarly fortifying properties. Judging from Madame de Pompadour as she downed her truffles and her celery soup, what was good for the gander must have benefited the goose, as well.

In addition to shape, the truffle's penetrating odor foretold its erotic powers. Connoisseurs have likened the scent to the tousled sheets of a brothel bed. Others, apparently drawing on a different set of life experiences for their analogies, compare it to melted Camembert or roasted garlic, while some insist it reeks of nothing but old bedding straw in a barn stall.

Pigs, who happen to dote on truffles, can smell them out from a hundred paces, and Europeans traditionally used sows to locate the precious mushrooms underneath the soil. During the seventeenth century, Italian gentry considered it great sport to set out strolling in the woods with a pig on a leash and a hired peasant walking a few respectable paces to the rear. When the sow picked up the scent of a truffle, she followed her formidable snout to the odor's source at the base of a tree, and eagerly started to grub about. The peasant then pushed her aside, dropped to his knees, and searched out the hidden treasure with a spade and his bare hands.

In spite of a very long list of testimonials in its favor, there is actually no definitive proof that a truffle acts as a bona fide sexual stimulant in humans. Moreover, says the FDA with hands on hips, the only aphrodisiac a person can really count on is the imagination. But there remains no doubt that truffles do the trick for lady pigs. Truffles contain a compound called androstenol, which is also found in the saliva of male pigs. In the boar, it serves as a pheromone — a scented hormone that an animal secretes to elicit a specific response amongst other members of its species. The effect of androstenol is to send the boar's inamorata into a fit of unbridled passion so that he may mate with her. Truffles contain this chemical in double the concentration possessed by the randy boar himself. Small wonder, then, Miss piggy takes off trotting when she catches a whiff of the mushrooms in the air.

It's not startling, either, that most truffle hunters now employ dogs to help them find their quarry. Canines have proved much easier to manage than lovesick sows, for they are highly trainable, their sense of smell is as keen as any pig's, and they are happier eating a dog biscuit than devouring a hundred-dollar truffle as a reward for their efforts. This high price tag, incidentally, offers yet another clue as to why the truffle's erotic powers became so celebrated. If ever there were a truism about aphrodisiacs, it is this: the more costly and rare they are, the wilder and more resounding the claims as to their efficacy.

Without a doubt, my own truffle purchase was a splurge. The mere buying of it was exhilaration in itself. The purveyor at the produce stall seemed certain that the excitement would only continue, for after she packaged it up, she clasped my hand briefly and said, "You take this straight home and cook it up for your man."

Who was I to argue?

My truffle came packed, in traditional fashion, in a cup of Arborio rice, which in turn had become infused with the mushroom's permeating odor. Italians use Arborio rice to create the classic braised dish they call risotto, which they usually serve as a first course in lieu of pasta. But I often make a meal out of it, along with a salad and a crusty loaf of bread. A truffled risotto, I decided, would be the perfect answer to the romantic meal I'd been ordered home to prepare.

So that evening, I started in by bringing a few cups of homemade chicken broth to a simmer on the back burner of the stove. Next, I pulled out a second pot, a broad, heavy one, which I employed to sauté a small diced onion and a minced clove of garlic in a little butter and a splash of olive oil over medium heat. I added my cup of rice, then stirred the ingredients around for a minute or two, until the grains glistened with oil and their rounded ends had become translucent. Then I poured in about half a glass of white wine, glug, glug, and I helped myself to a dainty tipple as well — risotto requires a great deal of stirring, and the cook who makes it deserves a little pampering, especially when that cook is embarking on as indulgent a meal as I had in store. After the sputtering wine had all but evaporated, I tipped in a ladleful of the hot broth, just enough to submerse the rice, and I turned down the heat a tad so the risotto would maintain a lively simmer, but not a raucous boil.

I continued leisurely tracing my spoon through the risotto, scraping the bottom and sides of the pot occasionally to keep the rice from sticking. Every few minutes, as the grains absorbed the liquid, I added another ladle of broth. As I listened to the risotto go plip, plip, plip, and as I stirred and ladled and sipped my wine, my thoughts turned to my truffle. It waited its turn for the pot in a tidy mound of paper-thin slices on the cutting board. Why, with its musky odor, it did seem to ooze promises of sensual delight. Then I started to compile a list. It was a list of potential stand-ins for my truffle, some succulent ingredients with aphrodisiacal tendencies of their own. Who knew how long it might be before I next found myself with a fresh black truffle in hand?

Seafood, in general, was first on my roster. Legend holds that Aphrodite, the Greek goddess of love who gave her name to all the foods and potions that stir up the soul, rose nude from the ocean on a bed of sea foam, and the ancients conferred her powers upon all variety of saltwater creatures. A medley of briny clams and mussels, and fleshy shrimp and calamari — surely these could match a truffle's strength, and they would make a fine risotto.

Oysters, on the other hand, belong on the half shell or in a stew, not in a risotto, at least in my mind. These mollusks do, however, reign supreme among seafood as enhancers of love. For many, their satiny, fluttered folds have evoked a woman's genitalia, and over the centuries countless people, especially men, have claimed that oysters drove them to distraction. Oysters were an essential at any self-respecting Roman orgy. To meet the demand, slaves packed these delicacies in snow and ice, then carted them overland from as far away as the English Channel. In eighteenth-century London, the prostitutes in upscale bordellos plied their clients with oysters to pique their palates and their ardor. Oysters appear by the platterful in the memoirs of the insatiable Casanova. He depended on these pearly mollusks to maintain his prowess with the ladies, and he found them exceedingly efficacious the time he nibbled them from the pursed lips of his two lovers.

It turns out these men were actually onto something, though in a roundabout, subtle sort of way. Oysters provide a hefty dose of zinc. This mineral is essential for the production of testosterone, the male hormone that regulates, among other things, a man's libido. Zinc also plays a role in the manufacture of sperm, and men who don't obtain enough of this element in their diets often have low sperm counts. Although you can find ample zinc in turkey sandwiches and hamburgers, a daily plate of oysters does have its merits.

Another arousing addition to my risotto would be a couple of generous handfuls of steamed, quartered artichoke hearts. Fresh would be best, but frozen would work if need be. This vegetable enjoyed a long reign as an aphrodisiac because of its alleged ability to heat the body. Until the advent of modern Western medicine, European physicians followed the teachings of Hippocrates and Galen and held that foods possessed properties to make them either cold, hot, dry, or damp. These traits produced various effects on the body. Cool, moist strawberries, for example, could help soothe a bilious constitution, while warm, drying teas of thyme leaves could clear phlegm from the chest. Artichokes were deemed hot, perhaps because they are actually the bud of a prickly thistle, and naturally, their inherent fire would cause the blood to smolder and arouse the passions. Garlic and onions had this attribute, as well, but they were too vulgar and smelly for all but the most crude and lascivious.

Catherine dei Medici could not contain her scandalous predilection for artichokes. She introduced them into France during the sixteenth century, packing them in her trousseau when she went off at fourteen to wed the future Henri II. At one outrageous affair, she stuffed herself with so many of these nasty novelties that the guests feared she might faint dead away, the little trollop, and disapproving whispers echoed for days among the more genteel ladies of the court.

Current science hasn't yet uncovered any evidence to support such steamy notions. Artichokes do have one physiological claim to fame, though. They are unique in containing an acid compound called cynarin (the artichoke belongs to the genus *Cynara*). The ability to detect cynarin is thought to be genetically inherited, and individuals who are sensitive to it will taste water as sweet immediately after eating artichokes. The chemical seems to stimulate the sweet taste buds and suppress the others. For what purpose, no one knows.

One of my favorite treats of spring is a risotto festooned with freshly shelled, blanched garden peas. But it is their leguminous cousins the dried beans that have the salacious reputation. They earned their renown not only with their supposed heating properties, but with their accompanying flatulence. The theory this time was that by causing such a commotion in the nether reaches of the alimentary canal, you surely must be titillating the more amorous organs housed in the same vicinity. Although they were vegetarians, neither Pythagoras nor his disciples would eat fava beans, which were the only beans known in the Old World until the conquistadors brought back the haricot and string varieties from America. Not only did these scholars believe beans housed the souls of the dead, they thought them dangerously stimulating. Likewise, nuns in some Italian convents were forbidden to eat beans, lest these prurient legumes provoke unhealthy carnal desires.

As a matter of fact, a steady diet of beans might garner a few positive results in some women, though nothing so immediate or bodice-ripping as the Mother Superiors once feared. The plant-estrogens in legumes are remarkably similar to the synthesized hormones that doctors often prescribe for women at the onset of menopause. Studies reveal promise that these plant-estrogens can provide many of the benefits of hormone replacement therapy without the cancerous side effects. Diets rich in legumes have been shown to alleviate the mood-swings, night sweats, and vaginal dryness associated with menopause, as well as to reduce the risk of osteoporosis. As for beans and their infernal flatulence, generations of Latin American cooks have countered the problem by putting a sprig of the herb epazote into the cooking pot. A pinch of baking soda in the soaking liquid seems to help some, too.

Although I've never tried one myself, a risotto garnished with frogs' legs is a specialty in parts of the Piedmont of Italy. European gourmands consider the amphibian quite the delicacy, and many a weary diner has sat down to a plate of these tasty appendages with hopes of acquiring in his own body the same vim and vitality his entrée once possessed in its muscular limbs. But as far as I know, medical journals have only twice linked frogs' legs to incidents of a lubricious nature, and even these were not without their drawbacks.

In 1861, and again in 1893, accounts appeared in the medical literature regarding French servicemen stationed in North Africa, who became ill after dining on frogs' legs. Both times, physicians diagnosed the soldiers' ailment as priapism, an excruciating, sustained erection of the penis. Their symptoms, the doctors noted, were not unlike those seen in men who had partaken too greedily in the drug cantharidin, a substance also known as Spanish Fly, which plays a naughty role in whorehouses as an aphrodisiac.

Cantharidin is extracted by crushing up a dried bug called a European blister beetle, and sure enough, when physicians dissected a frog from the same marsh as came the legionnaires' dinner, they found its belly full of these very beetles. Over a hundred years later,

Cornell researcher Thomas Eisner and his colleagues solved the case once and for all, demonstrating that frogs could indeed absorb the poisonous cantharidin into their muscles by eating blister beetles.

The drug acts to irritate and inflame the urinary tract. Without question, it will increase the blood flow to the penis or the clitoris for extended stretches of time. Yet I can't bring myself to recommend it. The fact that Spanish Fly is an illegal substance is the least of its shortcomings, as the drug can cause irreparable damage to the kidneys, even death. Frog's legs, on the other hand, are quite harmless, though I'd avoid any that leapt from North African ponds, just to be safe.

The grains of rice in my risotto were still hard as pebbles and, as sometimes happens, I'd almost run out of broth. It's difficult to tell exactly how much liquid you'll need in a risotto because you lose so much to evaporation during the braising. So I added a little water to the stock pot and continued stirring and simmering away. Although I hadn't planned anything for dessert, I did think of a couple of options that would have been in keeping with the evening's romantic theme.

A sleek box of chocolate truffles made an obvious choice, for the amatory powers of chocolate have been esteemed since the days of the Aztecs. Montezuma braced himself with a frothy chocolate brew, sipped from a golden chalice, before he availed himself of all the curvaceous, soft-skinned women in his harem. When Cortez and his men learned this, they held up their mugs for a refill, and once chocolate crossed the Atlantic, it earned the name *Theobroma cacao,* food of the gods. Untold paroxysms of ecstasy soon rippled through the regal courts of Europe, and in seventeenth-century England, the royal physician Henry Stubbs proclaimed in no uncertain terms that "chocolate is provocative to lust."

With its silken texture and its voluptuous way of melting on the tongue, with its intriguing bitter-sweet flavor, chocolate still has ardent fans who vouch for its stimulating influence. Most likely these people are feeling the small dose of caffeine — nine milligrams, or the equivalent of a few sips of coffee — packed into their Hershey bars. Chocolate does contain a substance called phenylethylamine, or PEA, an amphetamine-like compound that humans also produce. PEA's effect on the brain is to produce a surge of glorious giddiness, an emotion, chocolate fiends point out, that sounds an awful lot like the twitterpated feeling of falling in love. Unfortunately, the PEA in chocolate breaks down into a jumble of in-consequential building blocks in the stomach, so the active ingredient never makes it to the brain. Still, the confection is hardly wanting for sensual appeal.

Another qualified candidate for dessert would have been a spiced, honeyed cake, one redolent per-haps, of cinnamon, ginger, and cloves. Time and time again, fragrant spices and honey have made their way into the love philtres of history. The *Kama Sutra* devotes two chapters to the topic of aphrodisiacs. A good many of the recipes therein are rich with honey, hot with the likes of cardamom and nutmeg and black pepper, and full of promises to make a man enjoy innumerable women. No doubt the opium and the mountain skink, which is a stubby-legged lizard, were the active ingredients in a virility-promoting concoction hailed in the *Arabian Nights*. But the potion also called for peppercorns, cloves, cinnamon and ginger steeped in olive oil and honey.

Because it is sweet, and because it does not spoil, honey has received almost universal favor as a symbol of purity and well-being. Consequently, a spoonful of it was bound to do a body good. Until well into the eighteenth century, when refined sugar came into fashion, honey was the most concentrated sweetener available. This made it the best source of quick energy when it came to continuing the pleasures of the table on into the boudoir. People had only to blend it with a mix of exotic warm spices, which everyone knew would serve to kindle the humors and send the blood coursing fiery through the veins, and they would have one potent elixir.

More powerful still is the thick, milky secretion called royal jelly that the honeybee produces to feed the queen of the hive. At least that's what the product's proponents claim. Without her nutrient-rich, gooey meals of royal jelly, the mighty queen would have grown into nothing but a puny little worker bee, destined to toil away gathering pollen until her dying day. But look at her now! You need only possess an open, wishful mind to see the promise royal jelly holds in store for the human body. It turns back the clock. Erases wrinkles. Removes cellulite. And what it does for your nightlife, just you wait and see.

According to the man who tried to sell me some in Istanbul, however, I should have taken a dose much earlier in the day to reap its maximum benefits. My sister and I stumbled onto this fellow's stand deep in the maze of the Spice Market, where the air hangs sultry with the mingled scents of clove cigarettes and centuries of trafficking in cinnamon and saffron and turmeric. His tidy display of aphrodisiacs drew us in for a closer look. He offered two formulations: Sultan's Paste, for the man, and Harem of 1001 Nights, for the woman. Both were based on royal jelly. "Try some, pretty ladies," he said, pointing to a packaged box. "It makes you sizzle." He flashed a saucy grin that lacked two teeth. "All it takes is one spoonful before breakfast."

"Before breakfast?" I asked. "Why would I want to take it before breakfast, and then just have to go off to work?"

"Ah, yeah, yeah, that's my point. All day long you sizzle. Hot, hotter, hottest! Then, when your friend-boy, he come home at night, wow! It's unbelievable!"

and he smacked his fist into his opened hand to accentuate his point.

I'm sorry now I didn't bring any royal jelly home with me, because then I could vouch one way or the other for its efficacy. Undeniably, the stuff has some therapeutic uses. It is a source of B-vitamins, some amino acids and a few minerals, and medical studies have shown it can speed the healing of wounds. Daily supplements of royal jelly have proved helpful in reducing cholesterol levels, which may contribute to the overall health of the heart and the circulatory system. Since one of the leading causes of impotence is poor circulation, there is perhaps good cause to regard royal jelly as a promoter of sexual vigor. Even so, a bit of healthy skepticism remains in order as you listen to the stories of those who would have you buy their wares.

I could have gone on with my list for hours: goat's testicle, mandrake root, the grease of a gander, bat's blood, sparrow's eggs, the right lobe of a vulture's lung. These have all had their advocates over the years. Although it is hard not to dismiss such ludicrous drivel out of hand, you have to admire the determination and inventiveness of our forebears. One thing seems sure: hope has sprung eternal through the ages, regardless of whether any corresponding parts of the anatomy have ever been enticed to follow suit.

But a taste of my rice revealed it was almost tender to the bite. Some cookbooks lead you to think you can make a risotto with a stopwatch. Done in eighteen minutes flat. Remove from the stove-top after twenty-three minutes exactly. But I've found the only reliable method is to sample the grains after about twenty minutes, then continue with the braising and the broth ladling until the risotto has the consistency of very thick porridge rather than soup, and the rice has the lovely texture you would call *al dente* if you were boiling pasta. The finished product won't be at all light and fluffy like the rice pictured in the Betty Crocker cookbook. Rather, the grains will be bound to one another by the rich sauce they have created.

I took the pot off the flame, added a couple of handfuls of grated Parmesan, a nice pat of butter, some pepper and salt. Finally, I stirred in my truffle. I covered the pan and let it stand for a minute, which was all the heat the mushroom needed to release its full perfume. My husband tossed the salad and sliced the bread. He had the table laid out, the candles lit, a bottle of Barbaresco uncorked. We sat down to our meal, and the haunting truffle-scent rose with the steam from our bowls.

Although the chemists and the physiologists haven't succeeded in proving the poets right about truffles and romance, they haven't been able to prove them wrong, either. And of this much, I'm certain: there is something about a meal prepared with care and devotion, something about having a hand in the dish that will nourish both you and the person you love. There are indeed many ways to fuel the passions.

Daily Grind

AS A NATION, we have earned ourselves quite a reputation for pouring a lousy cup of coffee: *"Mon Dieu, quel désastre!"* What a disaster, a French teacher of mine once sighed, with a wistful tone in her voice for the *café au lait* of her native Paris. "You Americans, with your rush, rush, rush," said my host at an inn in Turkey, "all your coffee gives you is a kick." And, *"Che peccato,"* bemoaned the man who helped me catch a train in Bari. What a shame — the country that gave us blue jeans is such a bumbler when it comes to brewing coffee.

All this criticism might seem overly harsh or unfair, or at least out of date, for we Americans have come a long way since the percolator pot and ground coffee in a can. Our stylish coffee bars sport the sleek-est machinery and the most exquisite beans on the market. Commonplace now in restaurants and kitchen shops are thermal carafes and gold-plated drip filters, plunger-pots and frothing wands. Shiny espresso carts on city street corners flaunt shelves lined with bottles of colorful syrups and they stock plenty of dainty pas-tries to enjoy with your hot, frothy drink. Mention the daily grind, and instead of lamenting the drudgeries of nine to five, proprietors will pour you a sample of their freshly brewed Ethiopian Harrar or Brazilian Santos. And if you are having trouble with sleepless nights, they'll fix you a nice cup of decaf, for their spe-cialty roasters have Swiss-Water-Processed ninety-nine percent of the caffeine fears away.

Still, I've had bad coffee in meticulously ap-pointed stores from Boston to San Francisco. Sour coffee, made from stale beans. Burnt coffee, left on the heat-plate for hours. Flat cappuccino, drowned in scalded milk. I even had a tepid espresso in Seattle of all places, the coffee capital of the nation. I should have known, just by the sign in the window, that trouble lay ahead, because someone had spelled cappuccino with only one *p*.

For quite a while I was at a loss to explain the fact that so many of our so-called gourmet coffee establish-ments consistently fall short of the mark. Then I started paying attention to the goings-on behind the counter whenever I stepped in line for coffee, and the antics I witnessed spoke volumes. I saw waitresses pouring a ready-made black decoction out of a plastic jug, heating it, and calling it espresso. At another café, I watched a burly bald man garnish a cup of regular-strength coffee with a squirt of whipped cream from a can. "Here's your cappuccino," he growled, and I found him so intimidating, I didn't dare complain. And at one chic espresso bar, an overworked blond kid wildly scooped and spooned, tamped and frothed and pressed buttons, trying feverishly to keep pace with an impatient crowd. Single Mocha. *Macchiato.* Vanilla *Breve.* Make mine a tall one, extra shot. Panicked and besieged, he made two identical drinks. He held one of them out to a gentleman in line. "Would you like that, uh, decaf *latte,* with a sprinkle of chocolate or a dust of cinnamon?" he asked. Then he gave a nervous laugh and passed the next one off as a double cappuccino.

I came to see that the American coffee scene has mastered the ambience, learned the jargon, and turned itself into a hip new culture, but it doesn't seem to care enough yet about the coffee itself. Its purveyors have indeed done everything money can do to dress the coffee up. But a well-made cup requires a degree of attention and devotion that money cannot buy. And no amount of almond syrup or chocolate sprinkles can overcome this fact.

By way of contrast, consider the countries where coffee has a long-standing tradition as a social beverage. There, the priorities are rearranged. Substance takes precedence over form, and the drink has come to embody a way of life, not the latest trend. To illustrate my point, I could take you to a bustling café in Paris to read the paper and dunk a piece of baguette into the rich coffee-and-milk drink the French call *café au lait*. Or I could take you inside a Turkish home near Istanbul, where the method for brewing *kahveh* has changed little in over four hundred years. You could watch the hostess pulverize coffee beans by hand with a mortar and pestle, then brew them with sugar and water in a copper pot. Once, twice, three times she brings her *kahveh* to the boil, then offers it up in vase-shaped cups. But I am most familiar, and I must admit, most fond, of the Italian way with coffee. So I will take you to the Piedmont, to my Aunt Giuseppina's house. Hers is a minimalist's approach to the beverage. She gets by without hoopla or digital technology or even electricity, yet she manages quite nicely to brew up cup after soul-satisfying cup.

You might have been expecting me to say Giuseppina doles out espresso by the thimbleful from a rumbling machine on her kitchen counter. After all, Italians dote on the drink. You'll find an espresso bar in every city neighborhood and in almost every village in Italy — a place to congregate, to discuss soccer matches and politics, to play cards and watch the people go by. But espresso is a public beverage, and few Italians make it in the home. They recognize that a perfectly made cup depends upon a host of variables, chief among them a professional *barista*, or barman, with an experienced, attentive hand, and an immense, temperamental machine that cooperates only when it is as finely tuned as a concert piano.

So my Aunt Giuseppina brews her coffee at home on top of the stove in an eight-faceted metal contraption called a *moka*. The *moka,* which has been popular in Italy since the 1930s, is an hourglass-shaped, double-chambered pot with a filter nested in its middle. To use it, you heat water in the lower chamber, which causes steam to collect in the headroom. The accumulating vapor pressure forces the hot water out of the chamber, up through the ground coffee in the filter, and into the upper compartment, where it trickles forth, gurgling and spitting, dark and thick.

Many people call what comes out of a *moka* "stove-top espresso," and it is not everyone's cup of tea. When American store clerks are trying to sell you a two-hundred-dollar espresso machine for your home, they will sneer that the twenty-five-dollar *moka* merely makes weak, ersatz espresso, and they will scrunch up their noses at the mention of it. Their complaint is a matter of pressure. The espresso machine, popularized after the Second World War by a Milanese coffee machine manufacturer named Giovanni

Gaggia, has a powerful electric pump that forces hot water through powdered coffee grounds under immense pressure. The pressure breaks the coffee's oils and proteins up into tiny droplets, which disperse evenly throughout the water. This process, called emulsification, causes the brew to thicken, and results in the syrupy dram the Italians dubbed espresso because it is made "fast" and "to order." Compare this to coffee from say, a Mr. Coffee machine or any of the apparatuses that feature paper filters. They brew under the force of gravity alone. Drip. Drip. Drip. The flavorful oils from the coffee are extracted, but no emulsification occurs, and the brew lacks the heft and unctuous feel of espresso.

The steam pressure at work in a *moka* yields a brew that falls somewhere in the middle. It is thicker than regular coffee, but not so weighty as espresso, and Italians call it *caffè*. They consider it the perfect way to start the day and to finish the afternoon and evening meals around the table. To put the role of *caffè* into its proper perspective, it helps to know that Italians call their car *la macchina* — the machine. And they often refer to their coffee pot as *la macchinetta* — the little machine.

Giuseppina's little machine is actually not so small. It makes ten espresso-sized cups, which is just the right amount to serve the extended family that she frequently finds assembled around her table at mealtimes. I have a two-cup *moka* on the back of my own stove, and just listening to it hiss and sputter as it brews puts me back in Giuseppina's kitchen for a morning cup. As I emerge from her guest bedroom, the aroma of warm citrus envelopes me. I yawn, tuck a tress of my still-tousled hair behind my ear, and notice the strips of orange peel on top of her wood-burning cookstove. She has set them there to dry and shrivel like autumn leaves for no other reason than that their spicy scent makes for a pleasant way to meet the day.

"Ah, *buon giorno, carissima,*" she says from her seat at the kitchen table, her warm eyes lighting up. Giuseppina is not exactly my aunt. She's my mother's cousin, part of the family my grandmother left behind when she boarded ship for America. So Giuseppina and I are little more than shirttail relatives of some sort — first-cousins-once-removed, I think. But that is a connection far too distant to sum up the warm greeting she gave me when I first met her. I stepped off the train in Turin to tears and a kiss on each cheek and a spine-crushing hug that crossed generations and oceans and cultures, so that suddenly I'd known her all my life, and from then on she was aunt to me.

Giuseppina rises to her feet and smoothes her hand-crocheted woolen shawl over her shoulders. Soft white hair frames her high forehead, and dimples in her cheeks flash when she smiles. "*Hai dormito bene,* Teresa?" she asks.

"*Sì, grazie.*" I slept very well. I slept in a dark, cedar-and-violet perfumed room, tucked between sheets of fine linen. So even though I went to bed painfully full of Giuseppina's breadsticks and salami, and her prosciutto and roasted peppers, and ravioli and braised fennel, and veal saltimbocca and wilted greens, and apples and cheese and *tiramisu,* and seconds on coffee and altogether too much *vino rosso,* I awoke feeling surprisingly refreshed.

Giuseppina clasps her delicate hands together and says with animated anticipation, "*Vorresti un po' di caffè?*"

Oh, yes, I nod. Some coffee would be nice. I've planned to take a brisk jog this morning to ready my stomach for the *mortadella* and *vitello crudo* and two kinds of gnocchi and the rosemary chicken and parslied tomatoes and the apple tart that Giuseppina has promised for lunch. But perhaps a splash of coffee beforehand will help pick up my stride.

Giuseppina rinses her *moka* clean and fills its lower half with water. Cold springwater from the Alps. Some Italians believe the very notion of brewing good coffee outside their homeland is utter nonsense, for nowhere else in the world can you get such pure water. While this philosophy may be a bit extreme, it's true that brewed coffee is more than 98 percent water, and if chlorine or other off flavors overwhelm that water, a pot of coffee will be doomed from the start. Giuseppina may be blessed by geography, but the water filters now available at specialty coffee stores can work wonders for people whose tap water still tastes of the visit to the treatment plant.

Giuseppina fits the metal filter into the lower chamber's opening, spoons it full of coffee of a relatively fine grind, and tamps it lightly. If you asked her where this coffee came from, she would probable say up the road a piece, just past Barbania. She would shrug her shoulders at talk of Sumatra beans or Jamaica Blue Mountain, or Guatemalan Antigua, although American aficionados can chatter on about the subject until their coffee turns cold.

In the United States, coffee purveyors like to label beans by their point of origin. This is certainly a reasonable approach, for beans from different parts of the world have flavors that uniquely reflect the soil and climate of the lands in which they grew. Connoisseurs praise Ethiopian beans, for example, for their exotic, fruity taste. And they prize Guatemalan beans for their smoky, chocolatey qualities. But Italian roasters traditionally take another tack. They strive to create harmonious blends of beans, relying on one country's product for a little acidity, another country's coffee for its rich texture, and yet another's for its characteristic flavor. To argue that one method is better than the other proves only that it all comes down to taste, and everyone's taste is different. Giuseppina leaves the details of nationality to the owner at her local *torrefazione,* coffee roasting house, and a fine job he does in creating blends to suit her fancy.

Far more important than a bean's origin is its freshness. Although green coffee beans will keep for months and months, once they are roasted they quickly go stale and lose their flavor. They fade even faster once they've been ground, because a greater surface area is exposed to the air. This is why I consider an electric coffee grinder a kitchen essential. Giuseppina, however, doesn't go in much for gadgets. So, like most Italian housewives, she purchases her coffee beans in small quantities on the day they are roasted, has them milled on the spot, and uses them up quickly.

Giuseppina screws her *moka*'s upper compartment in place, then sets the pot on a hot spot over her stove-top. She leaves the lid ajar so she can keep an eye on its progress as she hovers about the kitchen, and when the *caffè* begins to brew, she moves the pot to a cooler corner of the woodstove. Giuseppina does have an electric oven, but she doesn't use it much, except as a place to dry and store her homemade cheeses. Ovens became fixtures in Italian household kitchens only after the better economic times that followed World War II. Prior to that, if you wanted to make bread or fix a lasagna, you took it to the village's communal oven or to the local baker. Most traditional family dishes trace their roots to the top of the stove, and Giuseppina is perfectly content to remain there.

In a few minutes, the sound from Giuseppina's *moka* turns from a hiss to a soft chortle, and she pulls the pot from the heat. It sputters for several more seconds and then falls silent. She fills two heavy, ceramic mugs halfway with *caffè,* then tops them off with a stream of the milk she has heated gently in a saucepot on the back of the stove. With a lilting, *"Ecco, per te,"* she places one of the mugs in front of me at the table.

Here, set before me, this steaming cup of morning wake-up-call, the breakfast beverage Italians call a *caffellatte*. The deep-roasted scent of it plays off Giuseppina's citrus peel from the stove in a contrapuntal aromatic symphony. I take a sip, at once soothing and invigorating, as evocative on the tongue as it is to the nose. It is this homespun drink that begat the stream of espresso-machine drinks that American shops serve up, all frothy and chocolate dusted, throughout the day.

Uncle Felice enters the kitchen, back from feeding dandelion greens to Giuseppina's chickens. He hands her two brown eggs, gives me a *buon giorno,* and Giuseppina serves him an oversized bowl brimming with *caffellatte*. She sets a tin of dry biscuits on the table along with a jar of her fig preserves — her Piedmont equivalent of morning toast and jam. Felice hums softly and holds a few biscuits over his bowl, crumbling them in with stiff, callused fingers. He gives the bowl a stir, then spoons up his *caffellatte* like porridge, while Giuseppina and I dunk and sip.

Soon, she notices I've emptied my mug. Surely I'd like a second cup, she says, she'd be happy to brew another pot. After all, I'll need it to accompany these lovely pastries she has, still warm from the bakery. And I must try her homemade apricots in syrup, she insists. *Deliziose!* And after that, how about a little sample of her sugared plums? She flits about the kitchen, opens cupboards, pulls out jars and bowls and spoons. Her *moka* starts to sing, and once again a heady coffee aroma streams from its spout. It looks like my brisk morning jog will just have to wait.

That afternoon at the end of the midday meal, Giuseppina brings out her *moka* again, this time for cups of what she calls *caffè corretto*. *Caffè corretto* means "corrected coffee." It is *caffè* with an added splash of liquor, usually grappa, an incendiary distillate of fermented grape skins, seeds, and pulp — the leftovers after making wine. Grappa packs quite a wallop, which is perhaps why Italians hail it for its therapeutic properties. It can cure a child of intestinal worms, they say, and it is a sure antidote for having eaten often and too well.

"*È un digestivo,*" Giuseppina explains, pouring a shot of it into my *caffè* after I finish my apple tart. A digestive. Felice leans forward and nods, motioning to Giuseppina that his own *caffè* could use some correcting as well. He lifts his cup to his lips and takes a sip. *"Buona medicina,"* he assures me.

And after supper there is that *moka* again, hard at work, brewing up *caffè* for us to drink black or to sweeten with sugar and sip from tiny cups. What pours forth from Giuseppina's *moka*, day in and day out, is by no means chic. It is not commercial coffee-bar espresso. It comes to the table in house slippers rather than in high heels, but that gives it a cozy appeal that I'll take over urban cool any day. For it is a classic beverage in its own right, and every drop of it reflects all the care and devotion that go into its making.

Afterword

A FEW MONTHS AFTER I wrote "Easy as Pie," December rolled around, and I gave a copy of the essay to my grandmother for Christmas. Toward the end of our holiday meal, as the bulk of Nana's clan was squeezed around two long tables, sipping coffee and polishing off the last of her date cookies, she asked me to read the piece aloud. I obliged, and began to recite my way through the do's and don'ts of pie-making.

When Nana realized she played a role in the story, she straightened herself up in her chair and pulled her sloped shoulders back. I could see her in the periphery of my vision, slowly nodding her agreement with each point I made: the butter should be cold. Yes. The water should be iced. Yes. It's best to make pies in the morning before the heat of the day sets in. Yes, indeed. But when I came to the part where I'd written, "Drizzle in the water and stir up the dough with a spoon," Nana piped in with a teasing scold, "Ah, honey, you use a fork!"

Later, in my own kitchen, I discovered she was right: the dough does come together more quickly when you mix it with a fork, which in turn helps to keep the pastry tender. So the final version of "Easy as Pie" contains that small but vital correction. And Nana's little reprimand offered me a taste of how simultaneously rewarding and humbling it would be to assemble this collection of essays.

When I embarked on this project, I thought I knew a great deal about cooking and food. In short order, I found out otherwise. And now, after spending countless more hours in the kitchen, after poring through the brittle pages of dozens of old cookbooks, and after observing cook upon fine cook at work at the stove, the realm of cookery has grown eminently more vast and rich for me. I've realized there's plenty yet I still don't know. To my dismay, I've discovered there is much that has been lost, as well, for historians have not always thought it important to record for posterity the goings-on of the kitchen.

What consistently struck me as I worked on these essays was the number of connections you can make, simply by cooking a meal. To prepare dinner for family and friends is to provide a reason for companions to come to the table at the end of the day and share — share food, conversation, laughter, tears. In fact, the word "companions" stems from the Latin, and it means roughly, "those with whom you break bread." To put together a pot of soup, a turkey stuffing, a pie, offers a link with the past, for diners have enjoyed these same dishes for centuries on end. And to uproot a carrot from the garden, or to wait impatiently for the June strawberries to ripen in their beds, is to reinforce a bond with the earth and its cycles — a bond that reminds us that food springs from the soil and the sea, not from plastic-wrapped boxes.

After I took my first kitchen job, I became most impressed with my newfound ability to carve tomato roses and make artistic squiggles with the crème fraîche in the raspberry purée. Fortunately, that phase was short-lived. Nowadays, I'm seldom enraptured by the adornments and the ado that surrounds so much of what goes by the name of fine contemporary cuisine. Which helps explain why I found myself drawn to the dishes in my essays: they represent a fresh, flavorful style of cooking whose vibrancy brings a beauty of its own to both the plate and the palate. And as I wrote, it became my wee amusement to point out just how often the chefs from the upper echelons of society have turned to the cooking of the working class for inspiration. While their own lavish sauces and fanciful dishes served well to demonstrate the extraordinary depth of their patrons' pockets, their cookery was less apt to give a diner inner satisfaction than it was to bring on indigestion or the gout. It seems that a desire to have food appease more than just the spasms of hunger in the stomach crosses the borders of every social class. On that note, this very moment I thought of another example and I can't resist including it:

My sisters and I grew up eating what we called "white spaghetti." This was during the '70s, when people weren't yet going around eating "pasta" for dinner. Your everyday spaghetti was red with tomato sauce, you had noodles for chicken soup, and you had macaroni for cheese and for casseroles. At our house we also had homemade lasagna and cannelloni and ravioli, and on Monday nights before my mother went out with her bowling team, we often had white spaghetti. She fixed it for us because it was quick, and because we all adored it.

To prepare it, my mom dropped a pound of spaghetti into a pot of boiling, salted water. While the pasta cooked, she rendered half a pound of diced bacon in a large frying pan, stirring it occasionally. Once the bacon turned golden and started to crisp, she poured off most of the fat and removed the pan from the heat. She broke three eggs into a small bowl and whisked them up well with a couple of generous handfuls of freshly grated Parmesan cheese. When the spaghetti was done cooking, she drained it quickly in a colander, then immediately added it to the bacon in the skillet. She drizzled in the eggs, added a liberal grinding of black pepper, and stirred continuously with a wooden fork for a couple of minutes until the noodles were well coated and their heat had cooked the eggs and cheese into a slightly thickened sauce. She poured the spaghetti into a serving dish, garnished it with additional grated cheese, then brought it to the table. We were soon too busy, the four of us, smacking our greedy little lips to bicker with one another or pitch temper tantrums as she scurried out the door, bowling bag in hand.

Some years later, I learned from a cookbook that white spaghetti has a real name. It is called *pasta alla carbonara*, and it is a standard fixture on trattoria menus around Rome. Debate abounds as to the origins of this name. Either it means "in the style of the charcoal-maker," and it was invented by coal men from the hillsides outside the city, or it is a mangled form of *carabinieri*, the Italian military police, and Roman housewives first made it for homesick American GIs during World War II with their rations of bacon and eggs. The American culinary forces have taken quite a shining to this dish of late; I've seen it featured on the menus of upbeat restaurants across the country. Just recently, a new acquaintance invited me to dinner. She had taken great pains with the evening's spread — brought out the silver candlesticks and cutlery, folded the cloth napkins into crisply pleated fans. "This," she said with a flourish as she served the main course forth from a Portmeirion platter, "This is *pasta alla carbonara*." So it was. My mother's white spaghetti. It certainly had done all right for itself since its coal-making or its soldiering days, whichever they were. And quite rightly, for it was delicious as ever; nearly as good, I'd say, as my mom's.

Now I want to come around again to polenta. At dinner one afternoon in the Piedmont, Uncle Felice heaped his plate with polenta and declared that as a youth he hadn't liked the stuff one bit. During the war, you see, there was nothing but polenta. Day after day, polenta, polenta. But now, with a slice of fontina, or a spoonful of Giuseppina's meat sauce, polenta was another story entirely. I had watched as Giuseppina prepared that meal, and she told me that some folks insist you should always stir polenta clockwise. Never the other way. But she herself did not believe it made a difference. "Oh, yes it does," Felice interrupted, putting down his newspaper and nodding with conviction. Giuseppina looked him in the eye, glanced at me, then reversed the circling of her wooden spoon. She began stirring to the left. Counter-clockwise. No need to guess who had the final say in that household when it came to matters of the table.

I must confess, I haven't put this polenta-stirring theory to the test. Every time I make the dish, I seem to find myself tracing my spoon in a figure eight before Felice's words come to mind. One of these days, though, I will remember to give his method a try, and I'll have a definitive answer to still another of my culinary questions. And who knows? Perhaps I'll find there's yet one more story in the polenta, just waiting to be told.

Recipes

Measuring Up

THE TIME HAS COME for a word about measuring. Within these pages I have measured in terms of handfuls and pinches and glugs and somes. I have used smidgens and drizzles galore. These are quantities that will make home economists across the nation wring their accomplished hands in despair, for they thought they had finally squelched such culinary vagueness.

Only in the last hundred years or so have cookbook writers placed a premium on precision when they recorded their recipes for posterity. According to the cookbook attributed to Apicius, you made Green Sauce for Fowl by combining "all kinds of green herbs, dates, honey, vinegar, wine, broth and oil." Instructions for a cheesecake in *The Accomplisht*

Cook, written by Robert May in 1685, call for a "pottle of curds, a good quantity of rose-water, crumbs from a small loaf of bread, ten yolks, and a good store of sugar." And to make a gooseberry tart, advised Amelia Simmons when she wrote the first American cookbook in 1796, "lay clean berries and sift over them sugar, then berries and sugar, 'till a deep dish be filled, cover with pastry, and bake somewhat more than other tarts." You would hardly expect such scanty directions from a lady who gave her cookbook the thoroughly descriptive title of *American Cookery, or the Art of Dressing Viands, Fish, Poultry and Vegetables, and the Best Modes of Making Pastes, Puffs, Pies, Tarts, Puddings, Custards, and Preserves, and All Kinds of Cakes, from the Imperial Plumb to Plain Cake, Adapted to This Country, and All Grades of Life, By Amelia Simmons, an American Orphan,* but that was the manner of the day.

Authors of books on cookery wrote for readers who were familiar with the techniques and the basic principles of the kitchen. For most cooks, recipes served primarily as aids to prompt the memory. What good would it do anyway, to write a recipe that required, say, three pounds of bone-in chicken breasts, when few homemakers possessed a scale? And why would a cook head out to the henhouse to sacrifice several birds, just for their breasts, when one chicken, cut into quarters, would suffice?

It would have been pure folly to instruct that these chicken pieces be combined in a large bowl with two teaspoons minced garlic, two teaspoons fresh thyme leaves, one cup onions cut into half-inch crescents, half a cup sliced, dried figs, half a teaspoon salt, one-quarter teaspoon freshly cracked pepper, three tablespoons olive oil, two tablespoons honey, one-quarter cup white wine vinegar, and one-quarter cup brandy or white wine, when very few cooks owned measuring utensils. Nor would it have proved one bit useful to the average housewife to say that the chicken should marinate one hour, for she hadn't a clock or a pocket watch or a timer in the house.

A home cook would not have found it helpful to read that the chicken and the marinating ingredients should be arranged in a single layer in a shallow pan, then baked for fifty minutes to an hour in a 350 degree oven. Chances were, she didn't have an oven, so she braised her chicken in a pot on the hearth or on top of her wood-burning stove. And if she did own a coal-burning range, it didn't have a thermostat. Experienced cooks told the oven's temperature by opening the door and quickly poking in a hand. Novices, advised my 1911 copy of *Mrs. Beeton's Book of Cookery,* should place a sheet of writing paper on the oven floor. When the paper's edges curl up and turn brown, the oven is hot enough to take a pastry or roast a fowl.

Far better, then, for a recipe simply to call for quantities like a cut-up onion and the leaves from a healthy sprig of thyme. And rather than stating a specific cooking time and temperature, it was much more practical to direct the cook to put a lid on the pot if the chicken seemed to be browning too quickly, to simmer the bird until its juices ran clear, and to serve the dish with roasted potatoes or buttered noodles.

At the end of the nineteenth century, culinary accoutrements became more readily available, and Miss Fannie Merritt Farmer decided it was high time such sloppy, freewheeling kitchen practices came to a halt. She took her cue from Mrs. Isabella Beeton over in London, who since 1861 had picked up the curious habit of including cooking times and accurate measurements in her books on household management. Miss Farmer approved mightily of this approach, and when she published *The Boston Cooking-School Cookbook* in 1896, she stamped her dainty foot and sternly insisted on standardized American measurements. Ladies, ladies, if ever we're going to get anywhere in the kitchen, then measure we must! Three teaspoons to a tablespoon, two tablespoons to an ounce, eight ounces to a cup. Hers became the protocol for all American cookbooks to follow.

Granted, something needed to be done to clarify the cryptic instructions that had prevailed for centuries. The home economists and chefs who did away with "butter the size of an egg" and "flour enough to make a stiff batter" have spared the world countless leaden tarts and fallen tortes, for pastry-baking is a game of ratios. It requires you to be most mindful of your teaspoons and cups, as there is no way to make adjustments after the cake has gone into the oven. When I bake, I measure with a conviction that would do Miss Farmer proud, and I specified level, exact amounts accordingly when I wrote of the likes of scones and biscuits.

But *cooking* is much more flexible and forgiving. Not to mention, there are fewer dishes to clean up when you count by tomatoes instead of ounces, and when you measure celery by the stalk instead of by the cup. The casual, family dishes in this collection do not hinge on precision in measuring for their success. They rely instead on fresh, pure ingredients, kitchen essentials like fruity olive oil, hand-grated cheese, and garden produce. They benefit immensely from a bit of patience and an occasional stir with a wooden spoon.

So now that you have read about my cooks who measure ingredients by eye and by the handful, feel confident that you can take out your pots and your frying pans and do the same. Recipes are not inviolable texts. They are guidelines, they are starting points. Take them into the kitchen and make them your own.

Stew and Polenta

FROM "PASS THE POLENTA" [PAGE 1]

SERVES 4

FOR THE STEW

2 pounds chuck roast or other stewing meat, trimmed
and cut into chunks
2–3 tablespoons oil or rendered fat from the meat
1 large onion, cut into thick crescents
4–5 small cloves garlic, peeled and slivered
1 bay leaf
1 good pinch each of oregano, thyme, and rosemary
1 glass of red wine
16-ounce jar of canned tomatoes, roughly cut,
including their liquid
2–3 stalks of celery, including their leaves, sliced
2 carrots, peeled and sliced
Quartered mushrooms, 1 cup or so, optional
1 turnip, peeled and sliced, optional
Salt and pepper to taste

Dredge the pieces of meat in flour. Heat the oil or fat in a
heavy stewpot. Add the meat and cook over medium heat
until the pieces are browned on all sides. Stir in the onion,
garlic, bay leaf, and herbs, and continue cooking until the
onion is translucent. Add the wine and tomatoes, and let
the stew simmer slowly, covered, for about two hours.
Check the pot occasionally and add water if the liquid has
evaporated. Toward the end of the cooking time, stir in
the remaining vegetables and continue braising gently
until the vegetables are tender. Season with salt and pepper. Can be made ahead and reheated.

FOR THE POLENTA

1 cup polenta (coarsely ground cornmeal)
4 cups cold water (you can substitute 1 cup stock or
   milk for part of the water.)
Salt and pepper
A few handfuls freshly grated Parmesan cheese

Stir water, polenta, and 1 teaspoon salt together in a heavy saucepan. Place over a low flame and stir slowly with a wooden spoon, scraping the bottom and sides of the pot to keep the polenta from sticking. Cook until the mixture thickens and pulls cleanly away from the sides of the pot, and the cornmeal feels tender on the tongue, 30–40 minutes. Stir in the cheese. Add freshly ground pepper and more salt, if needed, to taste.

TO ASSEMBLE AND SERVE AT TABLE

Put thin slices of mozzarella, provolone, and Gorgonzola cheeses on a serving plate — 8 ounces of cheese, total, is ample. Gruyère, fontina or Roquefort work well in this dish, too. Place the cheese plate on the table, along with the pot of stew and the dish of polenta. Diners serve themselves by spooning a mound of polenta onto their plate, followed by slices of the assorted cheeses and spoonfuls of stew.

Nana's Pie

FROM "EASY AS PIE" [PAGE 13]

FOR THE CRUST

2-1/2 cups all-purpose flour
Pinch of salt
Bigger pinch of sugar
1 cup chilled butter, cut into small chunks (for a flakier
    crust, use 3/4 cup butter and 1/4 cup shortening)
1/2 cup icewater

Combine flour, salt, and sugar in a large bowl. Work the butter into the flour with a pastry cutter or two forks. Mix only until the butter pieces are the size of peas, though a few lumps the size of small marbles are fine. Drizzle in the ice water and stir the mixture with a fork until it just starts to come together. It should feel like a handful of rich soil when you squeeze it. Form the dough into two disks, adding a little more water if necessary. Wrap in plastic or wax paper and refrigerate 20 minutes or so while you make the filling.

FOR THE FILLING

2 heaping pints blackberries, picked over for leaves and
    stems; blueberries are also nice
1/2 to 3/4 cup sugar, depending on tartness of berries
    and your taste
1/4 cup flour
Small pinch of cinnamon
Sprinkle of nutmeg, optional
Juice of a lemon
Grated rind of a lemon, optional
1 tablespoon butter, cut in thin flakes

Combine the berries, sugar, flour, spices, lemon juice, and rind, if using, in a large bowl. Let stand 10–15 minutes to let the juices come forth.

TO ASSEMBLE

Place one round of dough on a well-floured surface and roll into a circle 12 inches in diameter and 1/8-inch thick. Line a 9-inch pie plate with the dough, leaving edges untrimmed. Roll the second disk of dough into another 12-inch circle. Pour the filling into the bottom crust and dot with the flakes of butter. Place the top crust over the filling, trim and seal the edges, then make a crimped border around the rim. Brush the crust lightly with an egg-wash, made by beating an egg with a drizzle of milk, cut a few steam vents into the crust with the point of a knife, and bake in a 350-degree oven for one hour.

Many people who have read "Easy as Pie" seem to remember it as an essay about an apple pie, even though the filling has blackberries in it. So here is the way I make my apple pie filling:

FILLING FOR AN APPLE PIE

6 cups peeled and sliced tart apples (I like Northern Spy
   and Rhode Island Greening when I can find them,
   but Granny Smiths and Cortlands work well, too.)
2 tablespoons flour
1/2 to 3/4 cup sugar, depending on the tartness of the
   apples, and your taste
Juice of a lemon
2 teaspoons cinnamon
pinch of nutmeg
1 tablespoon butter, cut into thin flakes

Follow directions for berry filling.

Roast Chicken

FROM "A GOOD ROAST CHICKEN" [PAGE 27]

SERVES 4

---

1 four-pound chicken, preferably free-range
1–2 tablespoons melted butter or olive oil
Salt and freshly cracked pepper
1 lemon
3–4 rosemary sprigs
3–4 thyme sprigs
3–4 cloves of garlic, no need to peel

Rinse the chicken and pat it dry. Brush it lightly with melted butter (or use olive oil). Sprinkle it liberally with salt and pepper, inside and out. Place chicken breast-side up on a bed of rosemary sprigs in a roasting pan. Drizzle the chicken with the juice of the lemon. Tuck the lemon halves inside the bird's cavity, along with the thyme sprigs and garlic cloves. Roast in a 400-degree oven for one hour, until the juices run clear when you insert a knife at the thigh. Let the bird rest for ten minutes before serving.

Chicken with Figs and Fresh Thyme

FROM "MEASURING UP" [PAGE 237]

SERVES 4

---

1 three- to four-pound chicken, preferably free-range,
   quartered
2 cloves garlic, minced
2 teaspoons fresh thyme leaves
1 onion, cut into 1/2-inch crescents
1/2 cup dried figs, sliced
1/2 teaspoon salt
1/4 teaspoon freshly cracked pepper
3 tablespoons olive oil
2 tablespoons honey
1/4 cup white wine vinegar
1/4 cup brandy or white wine

Combine all the ingredients in a large bowl and let marinate at least one hour. Preheat oven to 350 degrees. Arrange the chicken pieces in a shallow pan, pour the marinade over them, and bake 50–60 minutes, or until the juices in the thigh run clear. Cover the pan with foil or a lid if the chicken seems to be browning too quickly.

Sauerkraut

FROM "OF CABBAGES AND KINGS" [PAGE 39]

MAKES 5-6 PINTS

TO MAKE SAUERKRAUT

5 pounds cabbage, as fresh as possible
3 tablespoons pickling salt

Wash a 1-gallon ceramic crock with hot, sudsy water, rinse it, then scald the insides with boiling water. Dry the crock with a clean towel. Remove the outer leaves from the cabbage heads, rinse the heads in cold water and drain. Quarter the heads, cut out the cores, and shred the cabbage on a grater or cut with a knife into quarter-thin slices (1/16 to 1/8 inch thick). Toss the shredded cabbage with the salt in a large bowl, then pack it in two-inch layers into the crock, pressing down on each layer firmly to release the juices. Place a sheet of plastic wrap over the cabbage. Fill a large, heavy plastic bag (a garbage bag works well) with water and set it on top of the plastic wrap, weighting down the cabbage underneath the brine. Tie the bag shut, and arrange it to form an airtight seal against the sides of the crock to prevent mold from growing. Put the crock in a cool, draft-free place until the bubbling stops, signifying that the fermentation is complete. At 70 degrees Fahrenheit, this takes 3–4 weeks. At 60 degrees, it takes about 6 weeks, but Nana says it tastes better. Pack into sterile jars and process in a boiling-water bath according to standard canning directions.

TO SERVE SAUERKRAUT WITH SMOKED SAUSAGES

SERVES 6

3 rashers bacon, sliced
1–2 onions, diced
2–3 cloves garlic, minced
1 quart sauerkraut, rinsed if not homemade
1 tart apple, peeled and grated
1–2 bay leaves
1 dozen juniper berries
Black pepper, to taste
1 dozen small red potatoes, halved or quartered
1 cup white wine
1 pint chicken stock or water
Smoked link-sausages, 2 links per person (Bratwurst,
    knockwurst or Polish sausages make good choices.)

Render the bacon over low heat in a large Dutch oven. Pour off the drippings, add the onion and garlic, and sauté until the onion is translucent. Stir in the sauerkraut, grated apple, and seasonings. Tuck the potatoes into the sauerkraut, pour in the wine and stock, and simmer until the potatoes just give way to a knife, about 30 minutes. Add more water if necessary. Sear the sausage links in a little oil in a hot skillet, then add them to the sauerkraut and let the kettle simmer for another 30 minutes, until the sausages are cooked through.

Thanksgiving Turkey Stuffing

FROM "THE SAME OLD STUFFING" [PAGE 51]

MAKES ENOUGH FOR A 10–12 POUND TURKEY

FOR MY MOM'S SPINACH AND RAISIN STUFFING

4 tablespoons butter (1/2 stick)
3/4 pound bulk sausage
1 large onion, diced
2 cloves garlic, minced
3 stalks celery, sliced
1 cup button mushrooms, sliced
1 pound fresh spinach, Swiss chard, or kale, blanched, chopped, and squeezed dry. Or substitute 1 box frozen spinach.
4 cups firm, stale bread, cubed
1/2 cup raisins
1/2 cup sliced almonds
1/2 cup freshly grated Parmesan
1 generous pinch each of oregano and rosemary
Salt and pepper, to taste
1 glass white wine

Brown the sausage in the butter over medium-low heat. Add onion, garlic, celery, and mushrooms, and sauté until cooked through. Stir in spinach and simmer briefly, just until heated. Let cool, then combine the mixture in a large bowl with the remaining ingredients. Fill cavity of turkey, or bake 45 minutes in a covered container alongside the roast.

FOR NANA'S SAGE AND ONION DRESSING

2 large onions, diced
4 large stalks celery, sliced, leaves included
2 cloves garlic, minced

1 stick butter
8 cups firm, stale bread, cubed
2 teaspoons dried sage
1 large handful chopped parsley
Pinch of nutmeg
Salt and pepper, to taste
3/4 to 1 cup turkey broth, approximately

Sauté onion, celery, and garlic in butter over a medium flame until tender. Let cool, then toss with the remaining ingredients in a large bowl, adding enough broth to make the stuffing hold together when you squeeze it. Fill cavity of turkey, or bake 45 minutes in a covered container alongside the roast.

Cioppino

FROM "WHEN FATHERS COOK" [PAGE 65]

SERVES 6

---

2 large Dungeness crabs, cleaned, cooked and cracked
  (You can substitute 3–4 Alaska king crab legs, 2
  lobster, or a pound of scallops.)
1 pound medium shrimp, peeled and deveined
1 pound mussels, scrubbed and bearded
1 pound steamer clams, scrubbed
1 pound red snapper or other firm-fleshed fish
1/4 cup olive oil
1 large onion, diced
2 stalks celery, thinly sliced
1 red bell pepper, diced
1 green bell pepper, diced
4 large cloves garlic, minced
Pinch saffron threads
1 teaspoon thyme
1 teaspoon oregano
1/2 teaspoon red pepper flakes
1 bay leaf
1 cup red wine
28 ounces canned tomatoes, roughly chopped,
  including their liquid
2 tablespoons tomato paste
3 cups fish stock (You can substitute chicken broth or
  bottled clam nectar diluted with water.)
1/4 cup fresh parsley, chopped
1/4 cup fresh basil, chopped
Salt

Heat the olive oil over a medium flame in a large Dutch oven. Sauté the onion, garlic, celery, and bell peppers until limp. Add crumbled saffron threads, thyme, oregano, red pepper flakes, and bay leaf, and cook another minute. Stir in red wine, let simmer a few minutes to dissipate the alcohol, then add the tomatoes and their liquid, the tomato paste and stock. Adjust the heat to maintain a simmer, then cook, uncovered, for thirty minutes. Stir in the parsley and basil, and add salt to taste. Put the clams and crab into the pot, and let cook 4–5 minutes. Add the rest of the shellfish and the red snapper, then return the lid to the pot. Continue cooking, shaking the pot occasionally, for another 5 minutes, or until the clams and mussels have opened, the shrimp has turned pink, and the fish has just cooked through.

FOR THE FISH STOCK

- 1–2 pounds assorted shrimp shells, crab or lobster shells, and fish frames (Halibut, snapper, and sea bass frames make good choices, but avoid any strong-flavored fish. Fish frames are usually available in the seafood department at your grocery store.)
- 1 cup white wine
- 1 onion
- 1 carrot
- 1 stalk celery
- 1 sprig parsley
- A few black peppercorns

Place ingredients in a stockpot. Cover with water, bring to a simmer, and let cook 30 minutes, skimming the scum from the surface occasionally. Strain. If you really want to do it up, cook the shells and frames in a little olive oil over medium heat for about ten minutes before you add the liquid. This adds a lovely depth of flavor to the stock. If you don't plan to use the stock immediately, let it cool to room temperature, then freeze it until needed. Makes about 1 quart.

Lena's Potato Rye Bread

FROM "YESTERDAY'S BREAD" [PAGE 79]

MAKES 2 LOAVES

FOR THE SPONGE

1 potato, the size of a child's fist
1-1/2 cups potato cooking liquid
1 teaspoon yeast
1/2 cup warm water
1 cup rye flour
1 cup all-purpose flour

Boil potato in a pot of water until tender. Reserve cooking liquid. Let potato cool to lukewarm, peel and mash in a large bowl, then stir in 1-1/2 cups of the cooking liquid. Proof yeast in 1/2 cup warm water until frothy, and stir into the bowl along with the flour. Cover with a towel and leave overnight in a draft-free place.

FOR THE BREAD

Sponge
1 tablespoon oil
1 large pinch sugar
1 scant tablespoon salt
4 cups all-purpose flour, plus additional flour, if needed

The next morning, stir down the sponge. Add the oil, sugar, and salt, and begin stirring in the flour, one cup at a time. Turn the dough out onto a floured surface and knead 10–15 minutes, until smooth and resilient, adding more flour if the dough seems sticky. Put into a lightly oiled bowl, cover with a towel or plastic wrap, and let rise in a warm place until double, 1-1/2 to 2 hours. Deflate the dough and shape into two round loaves. Place in lightly greased 8-inch cake rounds (or shape into cylinders and put in regular loaf pans). Let rise, covered, in a warm place until nearly doubled, about 45 minutes. With a sharp knife or razor blade make two slashes in the top of each loaf and bake at 375 degrees for 45 minutes, or until the loaves are deep golden and they sound hollow when you tap them.

Caesar Salad

FROM "ON TOSSING A CAESAR" [PAGE 121]

SERVES 4–6

FOR THE CROUTONS

2 cups day-old French bread, cut into cubes
Olive oil, a few tablespoons
1 clove garlic, minced
Pinch of salt

Put the bread cubes into a large bowl. Heat olive oil in a heavy skillet and add salt and garlic. When the garlic begins to sizzle, pour the oil over the bread cubes and toss to coat evenly. Spread the croutons out on a baking sheet and bake in a 350-degree oven until they are nicely browned, 15–20 minutes. Or cook them in the skillet over medium heat, stirring frequently.

FOR THE DRESSING

1 egg
Juice of 1 lemon
Few dashes Worcestershire sauce
2 cloves garlic, minced
4–5 anchovies, rinsed and minced
Salt, to taste
1/2 cup good quality olive oil

Combine all the ingredients in a bowl and whisk madly. Or, you can purée everything but the olive oil in a blender, then drizzle in the oil with the blender still whirring. This makes for a creamier dressing, but also for more cleanup. If you are bothered by the idea of the raw egg, simply omit it and substitute a half teaspoon of Dijon mustard.

TO ASSEMBLE

Rinse and pat dry a large head of romaine lettuce, tear it into bite-sized pieces, and put it into a large salad bowl. Add the croutons, along with a couple of generous handfuls of freshly grated Parmesan cheese and a few grinds of black pepper. Toss thoroughly with the dressing.

Potato and Leek Soup

FROM "NO ORDINARY SOUP" [PAGE 135]

SERVES 4

---

4 leeks, white and light green parts only, thinly sliced
4 russet potatoes, peeled and cut into bite-sized chunks
Light chicken broth or water, about 1-1/2 quarts
2–3 tablespoons butter
1 cup heavy cream
Salt and pepper, to taste
Fresh parsley, tarragon, or chervil, chopped, for garnish

Melt the butter in a large soup kettle over low heat and stew the potatoes and leeks a few minutes, until fragrant. Cover them by an inch with light chicken broth or water, add the bay leaf and 2 teaspoons of salt. Bring the soup to a boil, then turn down the heat and let simmer about 45 minutes, until the potatoes are tender. If you stop right here, you have *soupe à la bonne femme:* check the soup for salt, add a little pepper, swirl in a pat of butter and a handful of freshly chopped chervil or parsley just before serving. Or, purée the soup in a food mill or a blender, return it to the kettle, add the cream, and reheat over a low flame. Thin with more water if necessary and garnish with the freshly chopped herbs.

Currant Scones

FROM "A SECRET WELL KEPT" [PAGE 151]

MAKES 8 SCONES

---

2 cups all-purpose flour
3 teaspoons baking powder
1/4 teaspoon salt
3 tablespoons sugar
6 tablespoons butter, chilled, cut in pieces
1 cup heavy cream, chilled
1 cup currants

Preheat oven to 400 degrees. Combine flour, baking powder, sugar, and salt in a large bowl. Add butter, then toss with your fingers to coat each piece with flour. Work the mixture with your fingertips or a pastry cutter until it resembles coarse meal, with a few pea-sized lumps of butter still remaining. Drizzle in the cream, stirring the mixture with a fork, until it just comes together. Alternatively, combine the dry ingredients in the work bowl of a food processor, add the butter, and process with quick pulses until it is just incorporated. Add the cream in a thin stream, and pulse only until the mixture starts coming together. Do not over-process. Turn dough out onto a cutting board, sprinkle in the currants, and knead lightly, half a dozen times or so, until the dough forms a ball. Pat the dough into a circle 3/4 inch high. Dip a pastry brush into a lightly beaten egg and baste the dough-circle. Cut into 8 wedges. Transfer to a baking sheet and bake 12–15 minutes, or until golden brown.

Strawberry Shortcake

FROM "ENOUGH ROOM FOR STRAWBERRY SHORTCAKE" [PAGE 165]

SERVES 6–8

FOR THE STRAWBERRIES

3 pints ripe strawberries, rinsed, hulled, and sliced
Sugar, a couple of handfuls, or to taste

Toss berries in a bowl with sugar. Leave at room temperature for an hour, or until a syrup forms.

FOR THE BISCUITS

2-1/4 cups all-purpose flour
2 teaspoons sugar
2 teaspoons cream of tartar
1 teaspoon baking soda
A pinch of salt
8 tablespoons (1 stick) chilled butter, cut into small
    pieces
3/4 cup + 2 tablespoons cold buttermilk

Preheat oven to 400 degrees. Combine the dry ingredients in a large bowl. Work butter into flour with your fingertips or a pastry cutter, as you would for making a pie crust, until the mixture resembles coarse crumbs or rolled oats. Drizzle in buttermilk and stir with a fork, just until the dough holds together. Pat dough into a rectangle 3/4 inch high, cut into 6–8 rounds with a biscuit cutter or a drinking glass, or into squares with a knife, and transfer to a baking sheet. Even easier, and perhaps more impressive, pat the dough into a 9-inch cake pan and make one giant shortcake. Bake 12–15 minutes, or until golden brown.

FOR THE WHIPPED CREAM

1 pint heavy cream, chilled
Vanilla extract, 1 teaspoon, or to taste
Sugar, a spoonful, or to taste

Whip cream in a chilled bowl with a hand-mixer on low speed. When it begins to thicken, increase speed to high, add vanilla and sugar, and continue whipping until the cream holds soft peaks.

TO ASSEMBLE

Split the biscuits horizontally and spread with butter. Place the bottom halves on dessert plates and spoon the strawberries on top, including plenty of syrup. Put a generous dollop of whipped cream over the strawberries, top with the other biscuit half, and serve. For a special treat, serve while the biscuits are still hot from the oven.

Risotto

FROM "FUELING THE PASSIONS" [PAGE 193]

SERVES 4

FOR A BASIC RISOTTO

3–4 cups chicken broth; homemade is best
1 small onion, diced
1 clove garlic, minced
1 tablespoon butter, plus an additional spoonful for
    finishing the rice
A splash of olive oil
1 cup Arborio rice
1/2 glass white wine
A couple of handfuls of freshly grated Parmesan cheese
Salt and pepper, to taste

Bring the broth to a steady simmer. In a broad, heavy pot over a medium flame, sauté the onion and garlic in the butter and oil until limp and fragrant. Add the Arborio rice and stir until the grains become coated and their ends become translucent, 1–2 minutes. Pour in the wine, and adjust the heat to maintain a lively simmer. When the wine evaporates, add a ladle of broth. Continue stirring, adding a ladleful of broth each time the liquid is almost absorbed. After about 20 minutes, taste the rice for doneness, then continue braising until the grains are tender but firm to the bite *(al dente)* and the risotto has a thick, porridge-like consistency. Remove from the heat, and stir in a pat of butter, the Parmesan cheese, and salt and pepper to taste. Serve promptly and pass additional grated cheese at the table.

OPTIONAL ADDITIONS

If you find yourself with a fresh truffle or two in hand, a risotto would make a lovely place for them. If they are black truffles, slice them thinly, and stir them into the rice along with the Parmesan; this is all the heat black truffles need to release their flavor. The white truffle, on the other hand, is best enjoyed uncooked, so garnish the finished dish with thin shavings of it at the table. By no means should you let the fact that you are truffle-less keep you from making risotto. Like pasta, it lends itself to many variations. I think it best to keep any optional additions to only a few in number, because the dish can become too much of a jumble if you start tossing in ingredients willy-nilly. Steamed fresh artichoke hearts — figure on one sliced heart per person — are a nice touch, for example. Or steamed mussels, clams, calamari, and shrimp — about a pound, total; or a cup of fresh, blanched peas; or a cup each of sliced asparagus spears and morels (if you are lucky enough to find these wild spring mushrooms). Or a pinch of saffron, which is the classic Milanese rendition of the dish; or an ounce of reconstituted porcini mushrooms — whose soaking liquid makes a delightful addition to the broth. You get the idea. I find it easiest to cook these ingredients in a separate pot, then add them to the risotto near the end of the cooking time.

Spaghetti alla Carbonara

FROM THE AFTERWORD [PAGE 227]

SERVES 4-6

---

1 pound spaghetti
1/2 pound good-quality bacon, diced
3 eggs
A couple of handfuls of freshly grated Parmesan cheese,
   about 1/2 cup, plus more for garnishing
Fresh, coarsely ground black pepper

Cook the spaghetti in a large pot of boiling, salted water until *al dente*. Meanwhile, render the diced bacon in a large frying pan, stirring occasionally. After the bacon turns golden and starts to crisp, pour off most of the fat and remove the pan from the heat. In a small bowl, whisk the eggs and cheese until thoroughly combined. When the spaghetti is done cooking, drain it quickly in a colander, then add it immediately to the bacon in the skillet. Drizzle in the eggs, add a liberal grinding of pepper, and stir continuously with a wooden fork until the pasta is well coated and the eggs and cheese have cooked gently into a slightly thickened sauce. Pour into a serving bowl and garnish with additional grated cheese.

For Further Reading

I found myself turning to an eclectic mix of historical works, journal articles, essay collections, herbals, cookbooks, dictionaries, and encyclopedias as I went to research my stories. Among this lot, the following works struck me as particularly informative and entertaining, not to mention fairly obtainable:

Ackerman, Diane. *A Natural History of the Senses.* New York: Vintage Books, 1991.

———. *A Natural History of Love.* New York: Vintage Books, 1995.

Arora, David. *Mushrooms Demystified.* Berkeley, CA: Ten Speed Press, 1986.

Artusi, Pellegrino. *The Art of Eating Well.* Trans. Kyle M. Phillips, III. New York: Random House, 1996.

Audubon Society. *Field Guide to North American Mushrooms.* New York: Alfred Knopf, 1989.

Beach, S. A. *The Apples of New York.* 2 vols. Albany, NY: New York Dept. of Agriculture, 1905.

Behr, Edward. *The Artful Eater.* New York: Atlantic Monthly Press, 1992.

Brillat-Savarin, J.A. *The Physiology of Taste.* Trans. M. F. K. Fisher. New York: Harcourt, Brace, Jovanovich, 1978.

David, Elizabeth, *English Bread and Yeast Cookery*. London: Penguin Books, 1979.

Dumas, Alexandre. *Dictionary of Cuisine*. Ed. and trans. Louis Colman. New York: Simon and Schuster, 1958.

Fisher, M. F. K. *The Art of Eating*. New York: MacMillan Books, 1990.

Johnson, Hugh. *World Atlas of Wine*. New York: Simon and Schuster, 1985.

Kummer, Corby. *The Joy of Coffee*. Shelburne, VT: Chapters Publishing, 1995.

Lang, Jenifer Harvey, ed. *Larousse Gastronomique*. New York: Crown Publishers, 1990.

Mariani, John. *Dictionary of American Food and Drink*. New York: Hearst Books, 1994.

Morgan, Joan, and Alison Richards. *The Book of Apples*. London: Ebury Press, 1993.

McGee, Harold. *On Food and Cooking*. New York: Charles Scribner's Sons, 1984.

———. *The Curious Cook*. New York: MacMillan, 1990.

Rombauer, Irma S., and Marion Rombauer Becker. *Joy of Cooking*. New York: Bobbs-Merrill Co., 1975.

Root, Waverley, and Richard De Rochement. *Eating in America: a History*. New York: Morrow, 1976.

Root, Waverley. *The Food of France*. New York: Random House, 1971.

————. *Food*. New York: Simon and Schuster, 1980.

Sokolov, Raymond. *Why We Eat What We Eat*. New York: Summit Books, 1991.

Toussains-Samat, Maguelonne. *A History of Food*. Trans. Anthea Bell. Cambridge, MA: Blackwell Publishers, 1992.

Acknowledgments

COOKING IS AN EXCLUSIVELY human endeavor, a product of the hands and the heart. To write about cooking then, I found myself necessarily writing about people, and I owe a heartfelt thanks to all those who appear, often unwittingly, as characters in my essays. As for the writing itself, I only wish I could adequately express my gratitude. For their words of encouragement, their thoughtful suggestions, for their time and efforts on my behalf, I am grateful to Noel Perrin, Alan Lelchuk, and Barbara Kreiger. Especially Barbara, who ever-so-gently but firmly insisted on yet another revision, and without whom I doubt I would have seen this project through to completion. For their input on my early drafts, I owe thanks to the members of my writing group from the M.A.L.S. program at Dartmouth College: Alicia Green, Mark Laser, Carol Ehlen, Joan Kersey, Kevin Kertscher, Kathryn Niemela, Maggie Montgomery, and Rebecca Armstrong. And thanks to Bert, for proof-reading, and for letting me lie in bed in the morning until the coffee is made.

Index of Recipes

© Luciana Frigerio

A NOTE ON THE AUTHOR

Teresa Lust has worked in restaurants from the Pacific
Northwest to New England, and now lives in New
Hampshire with her husband Bert Davis. *Pass the
Polenta* is her first book.